SECRET SYRACUSE

A Guide to the Weird, Wonderful, and Obscure

Linda Lowen

Reedy Press
PO Box 5131
St. Louis, MO 63139
www.reedypress.com

Library of Congress Control Number: 2023938883
ISBN: 9781681064925

Design by Jill Halpin

Photo Editor: Sandy Roe/Photos at 1020

Unless otherwise indicated, all photos are courtesy of Sandy Roe or in the public domain.

Printed in the United States of America
23 24 25 26 27   5 4 3 2 1

To Mr. Green for concrete advice,
good spirits, and serendipity,
and to Jaye and Em,
twice the women I could ever hope to be

Skytop Quarry

CONTENTS

Onondaga Creek

ACKNOWLEDGMENTS

First and foremost, Photo Editor and principal photographer Sandy Roe of Photos at 1020 gets top billing because—since a picture paints a thousand words—she's contributed 1,000-3,000 words per entry to my paltry 300. In many cases, her photos came first and shaped how these stories were told.

Second, thanks to Debbie Horan who is looking at me as I write this and knows what's in my heart.

Third, valued readers Amanda Blue, Jim D'Aloisio, Kathy Miller, and Kelley Romano each contributed critical suggestions which made the work that much better. And special thanks to Dio Kaufman, who listened during the early stages of rabbit-hole research and rambling, ranting excitement.

Sharon Akkoul, Judy Carr, Chairish, Jim Farfaglia, Samuel Gruber, Mary Gualtieri, Brian Hamilton, Michael John Heagerty, Michelle Kivisto, Gloria Lamanna, Mark Murphy, Ellen Potter, Mary Salibrici, and Mark Sherlock selflessly provided suggestions, ideas, photographs, memorabilia, encouragement, and assistance.

The Onondaga Historical Association is Syracuse's best-kept secret since not enough folks know about, visit, support, and/or avail themselves of OHA's programs, downtown museum, community exhibits and on-site museums, and online resources and YouTube channel.

Thanks to Gus and Debbie for the time, space, and house in which to hunker down, work, sleep, rise, and grind—then lather, rinse, repeat for 48 days straight. As rocket scientist Robert H. Goddard said, "Everything is impossible until it is done." This is a tale of two cities: Our Fair City, the subject of the book, and Garden City, the coastal Carolina town where these entries were written. One could not have happened without the other.

Last and ever first in my world—Jim, Jo, Mia, Corrie, Max, and Jackson—thank you for adjusting your lives to the erratic flow of mine. You make me happy and, as John Crowley once wrote, "The things that make us happy make us wise."

World's Smallest Church

INTRODUCTION

Though this book is called *Secret Syracuse*, honestly, "secret" is a relative term. If the subtitle—*A Guide to the Weird, Wonderful, and Obscure*—pulled you in, know this: out of 84 entries, 29 are weird, 28 are wonderful, and 27 are obscure. Though they're short, just 300 words, each is a dense chunk of information. Spoiler alert: you will learn a lot.

"Weird" is a broad category and can include spooky, strange, and unsettling. A handful of those tales are here. Some will be familiar and may contain new information. Here's why: for every entry, I did a deep dive, often going back to original source material, including newspaper archives decades old. So if you're thinking, *but that's different from what I've read on the internet*, now you know why.

"Wonderful" is a matter of taste, but the root word is why I chose those entries. If you read something and want to visit it in real life—or find out more if it's no longer in existence—then you've experienced wonder too.

"Obscure" is the word that fueled the writing because obscure and secret describe what isn't well known. Secrets aren't always dark and hidden. Frequently, they're matter-of-fact, everyday, and in plain sight. But if everyone around you uses a word or phrase that you're unsure of, it's hard to admit ignorance. If I ask you "What is the Solvay Process? And which came first, the process or the village?" and you can't answer, don't worry. Neither could I before writing this book.

I've provided those answers in a short, easy-to-read format. Knowing the stories of the people and events that have shaped our fair city will have you walking these streets a little taller, a little prouder. It all happened, right here. Let's not keep it a secret any longer.

MISFORTUNE'S BEAUTY

Did a fortune teller in an East Syracuse railyard predict America's first supermodel?

Between 1909 and 1919, Audrey Munson's exquisite image was everywhere. Her face appeared on the half-dollar coin, and her figure inspired Manhattan's most famous statues. Depicted at the height of her fame, she still radiates serene perfection at the New York Public Library, from the peak of the 40-story Municipal Building, and atop the Pulitzer Fountain in Central Park. Yet in 1922, the *New York Times* reported that Munson attempted suicide in Mexico, NY.

Munson's tragic life had been foretold at age five, when her mother took her to a soothsayer in a seasonal Romany encampment in East Syracuse. The seer's prediction was ominous: "You shall be beloved and famous. But when you think that happiness is yours, its . . . fruit will turn to ashes in your mouth. You, who shall throw away thousands of dollars . . . shall want for a penny."

Born in Rochester in 1891, Munson landed in Manhattan in 1908. At 17, she began posing for painters, illustrators, photographers, and sculptors. As America's

AMERICA'S FIRST SUPERMODEL

WHAT: Audrey Munson rests here

WHERE: 4233 NY-104, New Haven, NY

COST: Free

PRO TIP: There is a historical marker at the cemetery, and a new headstone marks her resting place in lot 1 of block P28.

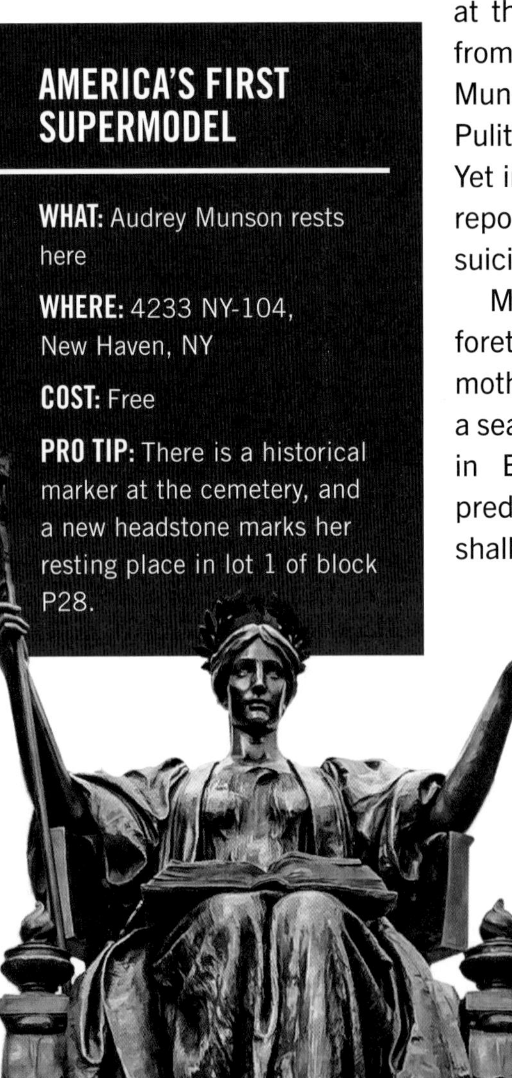

Alma Mater bronze sculpture, Columbia University.
Above: USS Maine *National Monument, Central Park.*
Inset: Audrey Munson. Courtesy of Library of Congress.

first nude film actress, she was a jet-setting movie star in the era of prop planes, and was flown to the set by Allan Loughead, cofounder of Lockheed Martin.

When a 65-year-old Manhattan doctor—infatuated with Munson—murdered his wife in 1919, her career nosedived. The next year, she moved in with her mother in Syracuse. Munson applied for work at the Syracuse Public Library but was turned down—and not just there but at 200 other places. Hoping to start afresh, she tried to plant her own obituary in a Syracuse newspaper. By her 30s, an erratic, reclusive Munson lived in a farmhouse outside Mexico, occasionally roller-skating into the village where locals called her "Crazy Audrey." She was committed to an asylum on her 40th birthday and institutionalized until her death in 1996 at 104. She's finally at peace in the nearby New Haven Cemetery.

An occasional newspaper columnist, Munson wrote about the fleeting nature of fame, wondering if readers ever asked themselves the question, "Where is she now, this model who was so beautiful?"

EIGHT IS ENOUGH

What prompted a Camillus farmer to build a healthy house?

Isaiah Wilcox was a man ahead of his time. More than 150 years ago, he moved from Rhode Island to Camillus, established a successful farm, and built a house so unique it's been restored and is now open to the public as a museum.

Wilcox was a staunch believer in the powers of an eight-sided house. The concept was championed by Orson Squire Fowler, a noted lecturer and phrenologist (one who measures bumps on the head to predict personality traits). Fowler felt the octagon house came close to the ideal of a circular human home. "Spherical is more beautiful than the angular," he stated, arguing that an octagon house offered more floor space and larger walls for windows. It also encouraged an "interchange of friendly and benevolent feeling." His ideas came together in *A Home for All: Or, a New, Cheap, Convenient, and Superior Mode of Building,* published in 1848.

That same year, Wilcox purchased the land in Camillus on which the house would later stand. Joy Flood, vice president of the Octagon House, says. "The octagon shape, he felt, was very healthy to the mind and the body." In 1856, he built his healthy home, replacing the original home on the property.

Inside the Wilcox Octagon House, you can still see his unique spiral staircase at the center—and climb its 62 steps, traversing six floors from bottom to top. The staircase begins in a deep root cellar and ends in a cupola that provides a 365-degree view of surrounding Camillus. With eight square

---

A deacon of the Camillus Baptist Church, Wilcox was known to be antislavery. The house's deep cellar is rumored to have been part of the Underground Railroad.

Tour the interior for a glimpse into the past. The spiral staircase is a unique feature.

THE WILCOX OCTAGON HOUSE MUSEUM

WHAT: An eight-sided healthy house

WHERE: 5420 West Genesee Street, Camillus

COST: Free

PRO TIP: Afternoon tours are held two Sundays a month, or you can visit during one of their annual events.

rooms, eight triangular rooms, and 10 closets, the house defies any expectations of pie-shaped rooms. At the time it was built, the house included no heat, hot water, light, or even a fireplace. Today, the house is on the National Register of Historic Places.

MAN CAVE MANOR

How did a 1930s bromance result in an English manor house?

They may have seemed an unlikely pair, the Columbia University sociology professor and the German artist who worked for Syroco, a decorative woodworking company, but Dr. William Casey and Severin Bischof were more than friends. They were imaginative visionaries whose whimsical collaboration produced the ultimate man cave hidden along the wooded shoreline of Lake Ontario.

Born in Moweaqua, Illinois, in 1891, Casey taught in a one-room schoolhouse and worked for a newspaper before earning his bachelor's degree in 1916 and his PhD in 1926. Though he joined the sociology department at Columbia in 1931, he briefly taught at Syracuse University (SU).

Bischof was born in Wenden, Germany, in 1893, to a master mason. Apprenticed to his father, he worked across Europe on grand cathedrals. He restored religious paintings, cut glass, and eventually became a master painter. Arriving in New York in 1924, he met Casey in 1928 while an art student at SU.

Casey had been a frequent summer visitor to an elegant Lake Ontario resort, the Mexico Point Clubhouse. A former carriage house on the property intrigued him; Casey envisioned it as an 11th-century English manor house and convinced Bischof to lend his talents.

In the 1930s, aided by friends and students, they installed stained glass windows, creating a Great Hall with a majestic stone fireplace. Walls bore carvings of knights, clergy, nobility, and

Detailed craftsmanship throughout the cottage.

the overhead beams featured lines from Chaucer's *Canterbury Tales*. Casey's Cottage was "a work of love, a place of beauty, friends, companionship and good conversation only," according to Bischof's son John.

Upon Casey's death in 1978, the cottage was abandoned, but it's been restored and is now open to visitors. While the Mexico Point Clubhouse was lost in a fire, Casey's Cottage was untouched, and it's now part of Mexico Point State Park.

CASEY'S COTTAGE AT MEXICO POINT STATE PARK

WHAT: A carriage house reimagined as an English manor house

WHERE: Mexico Point Park, County Rte. 40, Mexico, NY

COST: Free

PRO TIP: The cottage is open on weekends May-September, and it can be rented out at other times for events of 50 people or fewer.

Casey's Cottage is rumored to be haunted, with park volunteers and paranormal investigators reporting a variety of phenomena, including orbs, voices, and shadows.

BEST OF THE REST

What "presidential" luxury item was associated with Syracuse?

For more than a century, the Rolls-Royce of caskets was assembled by hand in Syracuse at the Marsellus Casket Company. The family-owned business produced the world's finest hardwood caskets for prominent individuals, including US Presidents Harry Truman, Richard Nixon, Ronald Reagan, and John F. Kennedy.

Hand-carved surfaces; velour, crepe, and velvet interiors; brass screws; and solid woods distinguished a Marsellus casket. The company was the first to use copper and zinc to line its caskets. Each took months to build. Sixteen hours of hand polishing resulted in what the company called "the mirror-like Marsellus reflection of perfection." The legendary craftsmanship was driven by founder John Marsellus's belief, "Never compromise quality. Build your product up to a standard, not down to a price."

Marsellus was a traveling salesman of undertaker supplies when he hopped off an Erie Canal boat in Syracuse. "This is a bustling community," he wrote in his diary. He not only stayed, but founded a company in 1872 to produce broomsticks, novelties, medicine chests, and shoe brush handles, along with caskets. In 1887, Marsellus purchased a lot on Richmond Avenue and, two years later, built a four-story, 70,000-square-foot factory that was one of the biggest buildings between Albany and Buffalo. In 1990, another factory was built in Dewitt.

Marsellus was a forward-thinking employer, recognizing "the immortal worth and dignity of . . . all men—even those performing the most humble of tasks . . . and that all work is glorified."

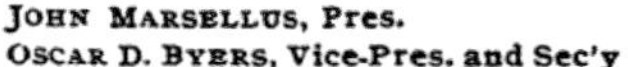

CHAS. B. KIGGINS, Treas.
JOHN C. MARSELLUS, Asst Sec.

John Marsellus Mfg. Co.

Manufacturers of

Coffins, Caskets and Undertakers' Sundries

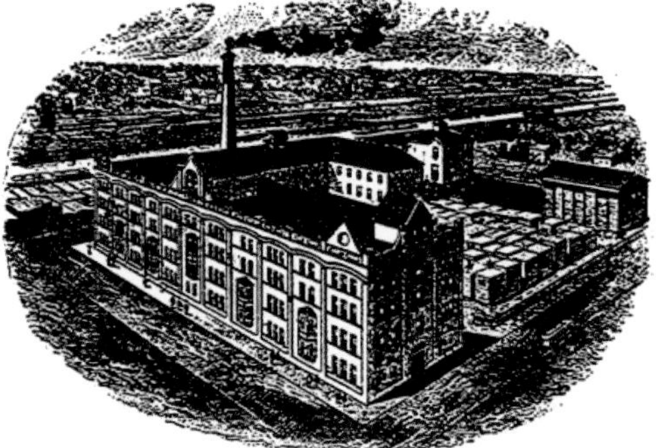

Wholesale Dealers in

Cabinet Hardware Upholstery Goods, Etc.

No Better Plant or Product to be Found Anywhere in the United States

FACTORY, SALESROOM AND OFFICE

Cor. Van Rensselaer, Richmond and Tracy Sts., Syracuse, N. Y.

Early print advertisement. Public domain

Marsellus employed immigrants from Germany, Italy, Poland, Portugal, Vietnam, and Bosnia. Many workers were from the same family and spent their entire working lives at the company, which regarded its fabric cutters, sewers, upholsterers, woodworkers, and cabinet makers "not [as] an assembly line but an assembled group of skilled workers."

Four generations led the family-owned company until it was sold in 1997. In 2003, the new owner ended Syracuse manufacturing and sold the patents, copyright, and name to a rival casket company.

MARSELLUS CASKET COMPANY

WHAT: The Rolls-Royce of Caskets

WHERE: Rebuilt as Marsellus Commons, 101 Richmond Avenue

COST: Free

PRO TIP: John Marsellus's final resting place is in Oakwood Cemetery, Sect. B, Plot 136, where he was undoubtedly interred in one of his company's caskets.

ACCIDENTAL CASKET OF CAMELOT

Why was JFK returned to DC in one casket and buried in another?

John F. Kennedy's iconic years in the White House—what his widow Jackie called the Thousand Days of Camelot—ended with an unfortunate event tied to Syracuse: his burial in a Marsellus Casket. Painstakingly constructed by hand to exacting standards at the company's 101 Richmond Street factory, the expensive casket—which would have cost $31,000 today was actually not the first choice of repose.

On the day Kennedy was assassinated in November 1963, a Secret Service agent called a Dallas funeral home requesting the best available casket be delivered to the hospital where the president had been taken. What arrived was a Handley Britannia from the Elgin Casket Company, a $3,995 solid bronze coffin with white satin lining. To protect the casket during the flight back to Washington, the president's head wounds were carefully wrapped.

Upon arrival, he was brought to Bethesda Naval Hospital for an autopsy prior to embalming. But

JFK'S MARSELLUS CASKET

WHAT: A second-choice casket fit for a president

WHERE: Hand-assembled at 101 Richmond Street, it's now in Arlington National Cemetery

COST: Free

PRO TIP: A few Syracuse-produced original Marsellus caskets are still available, but it'll set you back five figures.

Upon Jackie's death, she too was buried in a Marsellus casket, this time by choice.

JFK casket carried up the steps of the Capitol. Courtesy of Wikimedia Commons.

in transit, the casket lining had become blood-soaked, rendering it unusable for the public observances that lay ahead.

According to historian Anthony Bergen, a mortuary team from Gawler's Funeral Home embalmed the president's body, laying him in a Marsellus 710 coffin crafted from "hand-rubbed, five-hundred-year-old African mahogany"—price tag: $3,160. Over the next three days—from the White House East Room to the Capitol Rotunda and the funeral at St. Matthew's Cathedral—that Marsellus casket was the focus of worldwide grief: "It was that flag-draped casket from Gawler's that John F. Kennedy Jr. saluted and Americans saw being laid to rest in Arlington National Cemetery."

When Marsellus ended casket manufacturing in Syracuse in 2003, the last one produced was a model 710 casket designated "The President," featuring mahogany wood and a pearl-colored velvet lining. It's at the National Museum of Funeral History in Houston.

RULER OF THE PALACE

Where was the "Queen of the Neighborhood Silver Screens"?

In 1924, when a business block of storefronts opened in the village of Eastwood, a "picture show" was smack dab in the middle. Over the next hundred years, as businesses came and went and the village was annexed by Syracuse, The Palace Theatre remained a constant in what is now the Eastwood neighborhood. Alfred DiBella was the owner. An Italian immigrant, DiBella had been in the US less than two decades when he developed the corner lot at James Street and Stafford Avenue; it was "swampy, with a bit of a slope" wrote Dick Case, Syracuse newspaper columnist and author of *Remembering Syracuse*.

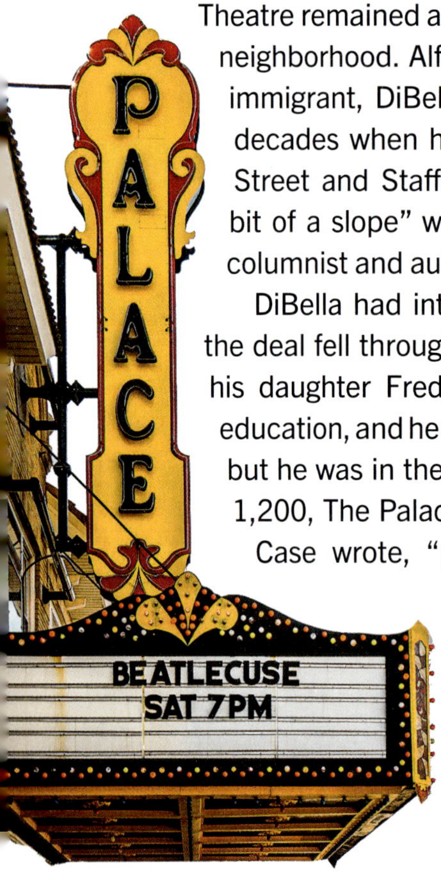

DiBella had intended to lease the movie house but the deal fell through, leaving him to run it, and "he did," his daughter Freda told Case. "He didn't have much education, and he spoke broken English in the beginning, but he was in the theater business." With a capacity of 1,200, The Palace was the center of Eastwood where, Case wrote, "people could watch a movie or an amateur show and, in the old days, win a set of dishes, a bicycle, a bag of coins, or a bingo jackpot."

After Alfred died in 1959, daughter Frances bought the picture show from her mother. Known as "The lady at the

Over the decades that DiBella's daughter Frances ruled The Palace while films flickered inside the theater, she admitted to liking *Gone with the Wind* but said, "most of the time, I read."

The bold marquee of The Palace Theater hearkens back to an earlier time.

Palace," Frances was an astute businesswoman, running the movie theater almost singlehandedly for decades. She took tickets and sold popcorn. Though she stooped more as she grew older, Frances was fierce and formidable. In his column, Case advised, "[D]on't talk during the show or put your feet on the seat ahead or the boss with be there with a flashlight, threatening to call the cops." In her 2004 obituary, Frances DiBella was cited as "one of the few women in a business mostly run by large corporations."

FRANCES DIBELLA AND THE PALACE THEATRE

WHAT: The proprietress behind Eastwood's independent movie theater

WHERE: 2384 James Street

COST: Variable pricing

PRO TIP: Operating primarily as an event/concert space, The Palace now seats up to 500.

WOODEN IT BE NICE

What former Syracuse decorative manufacturer still trends on TikTok?

Even though their Syracuse factory closed in 2007, the sun never sets on Syroco, a company whose many products still surface in thrift stores, resale shops, and online. Associated with Maximalist and Hollywood Regency decor, the elaborate designs—featuring scrollwork, sunbursts, garlands, florals, and even peacocks—elicit a "love it or leave it" response. Upcycled furniture fans grab it cheap for makeovers they share on social media. Search out #syroco on TikTok; you'll be one of 420,000 viewers. A wide variety of folks—mid-century modernists, Halloween horror enthusiasts, starburst clock collectors, and those who "want home to feel like Versailles"—gravitate to Syroco.

Grace Wagner, formerly with the Special Collections Research Center at Syracuse University Libraries, understands. She admits, "my affinity for Syroco comes from years of discovering the . . . logo on the back of estate and garage sale finds." She's praised Syroco's "astounding ability to invent and reinvent itself numerous times over more than a century of business," noting "each era of production is marked by certain hallmarks . . . [providing] an interesting benchmark for trends and progress over time."

An acronym for **Syr**acuse **O**rnamental **Co**mpany, Syroco was started in 1890 by Austrian immigrant Adolph Holstein to produce hand-carved decorative wood items. Early catalogs contained everything from simple moldings to elaborate

SYROCO

WHAT: Decorative goods resembling carved wood

WHERE: Formerly at 581 South Clinton Street

COST: Cheap at thrift stores

PRO TIP: More than 10,000+ pieces are available online: 4,000 on Etsy, 7,200 on eBay, plus quality Syroco from high-end resellers such as Chairish.

Courtesy of Chairish.com and Scranton Antiques.

scrollwork. In 1923, Syroco began offering a new "90% wood product": SyrocoWood, Adirondack wood pulp mixed with flour and other materials. Extruded, molded, and dried, it was finished to look like wood or painted. Syroco's novelty items in the 1930s and 1940s included manly goods such as shaving kits, tie holders, and cigar boxes. In 1968–69 they launched Lady Syroco home products to capture female consumers. Yet, like other Syracuse manufacturers, changes in the economic landscape led to declining sales and an end to local production.

Plastics helped and hurt Syroco. Injection molding arrived in the 1960s, and a Baldwinsville plant opened in 1963 for PVC and polystyrene. In the end, Syroco made patio furniture.

HAUNTED OR PUNK'D?

How did the story of Thirteen Curves get its start?

Widely known as Thirteen Curves, Cedarvale Road is allegedly where a ghostly bride searches for her groom. Both died on their wedding night when their vehicle slid off the road while negotiating its treacherous turns. Accounts of the time frame vary—some say they drove a horse and buggy, others insist it was an automobile—but the woman in white has never been in dispute. It's Central New York's preeminent ghost story. Yet just like Ashton Kutcher's MTV reality show *Punk'd*, it may be one big practical joke.

In an October 2000 Associated Press story, a Chittenango woman named Anita Popluhar revealed the story was a hoax. According to the article, "Popluhar, 58, grew up on the corner of Cedarvale and Pleasant Valley Roads and later bought her parents' home. She never heard the tale in all her years growing up there. In the early 1970s . . . she and her ex-husband employed twin baby sitters who had boyfriends from Syracuse." To prank the girls, she made up the wedding-night story then, draped in a white sheet and bearing a flashlight, she climbed the hill behind her barn and "scared the bejeebers out of the city kids . . . Prior to that time, there was never any story."

Yet Nedrow resident Angie Styb swears on Halloween 1998 she saw a milky white figure on a hillside above Thirteen Curves holding a glowing lantern. It was "exciting, shocking, exhilarating . . . frightening," and real to Styb who argued, "no way someone could have set that up." Clay resident Dolores Collard remembers how, at age 12 in the 1950s, "a beautiful

---

While a visit at any time of year will send chills down your spine, a Halloween drive is rumored to be the most opportune time to see the bride.

Snow and ice add a different element of fear to this winding road. Inset courtesy of Linda Lowen.

woman in a white gown walked right through the car" she was riding in. Collard claimed, "You could feel her presence and everything."

It's said that truth is a moving target. A historical marker honoring Thirteen Curves pays tribute to the legend, regardless of its source.

THIRTEEN CURVES

WHAT: A ghostly bride searches for her dead husband

WHERE: Cedarvale Road and West Seneca Turnpike

COST: Free

PRO TIP: The actual location of the alleged accident is also up for debate. Some say it's Curve #6; others say #7.

OFF THE RAILS

Where can visitors relive the Golden Age of Railroads?

You're never too old for trains—or the nostalgic lure of a quaint rural railroad station. Before airplanes, before automobiles, imagine what it must have been like to sit on a carved wooden bench in a waiting room warmed by a pot-bellied stove, anticipating your journey by railway after handing your pennies over at the ticket window to purchase your first train ticket.

If your imagination fails you, you can come close to experiencing the real thing at the Martisco Station Museum. Just north of Marcellus, the museum is housed in a former New York Central Railroad station built in 1870. This charming two-story building with brickwork painted mint and forest green is an eye-catching structure on the outside with even greater surprises inside.

The Victorian-style station closed after passenger train service to Martisco ended in 1958. It was boarded up in 1960, but after the Central New York Chapter of the National Railway Society purchased the station, it came back to life as a museum. The first floor has been restored to replicate its original use, giving visitors a sense of what passengers might have experienced during the heyday of the US railway system. The second floor houses railroad exhibits of interest to adults and children.

MARTISCO STATION MUSEUM

WHAT: A restored 1870 station time capsule of railway history

WHERE: 5085 Martisco Road, Marcellus

COST: Free to visit Sunday afternoons May-October

PRO TIP: The gift shop has train-related goods, including replicas of the iconic hat worn by Mr. Conductor (played by Ringo Starr, George Carlin, and CNY favorite Alec Baldwin) on the children's TV series, *Shining Time Station.*

Plan your visit to coincide with the museum's hours of operation. Top right and above center courtesy of Central New York Chapter National Railway Historical Society.

Next door, the abandoned Martisco Station agent's living quarters are now home to the Chapter's library, open to researchers by appointment.

In 2007, due to its historic architecture and cultural significance, Martisco Station was added to the National Register of Historic Places.

THE GREATEST SHOWMAN

Did Syracuse once have its very own circus?

For half a century, a flamboyant showman filled seats—and moved mountains of performers, equipment, and animals—for his Big Shows operating out of Syracuse. Using wagons, boats, trains, and trucks like comedian John Candy in the 1987 film *Planes, Trains, and Automobiles*, Sig Sautelle tried every mode of transportation to get himself—and his circus—from here to there.

The performing bug bit 12-year-old George Satterly during the Civil War. He left the Adirondacks, enlisting in the Union army as a drummer boy. There, he learned showbiz tricks from a ventriloquist. By 21, George was a sideshow magician, ventriloquist, and puppeteer, yet writer Curtis Harris said, "He saw himself as a great Italian circus star and so changed his name . . . to Signor Sautelle."

In 1875, at 25, he bought a blind horse, a harness, and a wagon for $23—not an auspicious start. Yet, in 1882, he opened Sig Sautelle's Big Shows in Syracuse. His circus traveled by boat to perform in towns along the Erie Canal and other waterways.

Sautelle wintered in Syracuse, often staging Punch and Judy shows; the *Syracuse Herald* described a Thanksgiving performance attended by thousands of children. In 1887, he traded boats for wagons. Circus historian John C. Kunzog noted that in 1891 Sautelle "had 225 people on the payroll, boasted two elephants, 14 cages of animals and 150 head of horses and

---

Part of Sig Sautelle's fortune went into the construction of an unusual octagonal house in Homer, NY—known as the Circus House—that's still standing today.

A look back at Syracuse's legendary circus and its bigger-than-life impresario. Courtesy of New York Public Library.

ponies." Quite wealthy by 1902, he pivoted again, this time from roadways to rail lines, buying flat cars to travel by train.

A decade later, the money was gone. His wife's worsening health forced him to sell the circus. His bankruptcy in 1914 and her death in 1916 ended his career. Though he tried to launch a circus truck show in 1927, after failing yet again, Sautelle died in June 1928.

SIG SAUTELLE

WHAT: A Syracuse-based circus showman

WHERE: An old car barn on Grape Street (now Townsend)

COST: Free

PRO TIP: Though the big-top splendor of Sig Sautelle's Circus is long gone, the New York Public Library's digital collections contain several photos.

UNDER THE BIG TOP

Why was a house built specifically for circus animals?

When he started his business in 1882, Syracuse circus impresario Sig Sautelle needed dozens of animals for his Big Shows, both working domestic beasts and exotics such as tigers, elephants, and lions. They earned him money while touring, but the off season was a challenge. For two decades, Syracuse had been his home base, and his animals had been housed in an old car barn on Grape Street (now Townsend Avenue), but after the building's sale, he was told to vacate.

After briefly relocating to Deruyter, Sautelle chose Homer as his winter home. Fortunately, the circus had made Sautelle a very wealthy man, so he bought two hotels for his circus performers and workers. He also began to introduce into the rural landscape what circus historian John C. Kunzog called "his bizarre style of architecture—octagonal-shaped buildings—resembling as near as possible a circus tent." Sautelle eventually built three of these circus houses in Homer: "The large animal barn was the first...to be erected; the training stables followed. Sig . . . was so pleased with his accomplishments as an architect that he promptly proceeded to draw plans for an octagonal-shaped dwelling."

The building timeline was in dispute among locals. Kunzog noted, "Some state that Sig razed the animal barn to build the house; others aver that all three octagonal structures were standing at the

CIRCUS HOUSE

WHAT: An octagonal house designed to resemble a circus tent

WHERE: 159 South Main Street (US 11), Homer

COST: Free to view from the outside (privately owned)

PRO TIP: Downtown Homer is a charming village with shopping, dining, and lovely homes—well worth a visit on its own.

same time, and that a windstorm razed the animal barn." Both the structures and the creatures they housed drew attention. In warmer months, the animals were outside like ordinary livestock: "Elephants grazing on the hillside was a familiar sight."

Today, only one of the three structures remains, and it is in dilapidated condition after housing a diner and then an antique store. While it's believed this was Sautelle's home, that too is uncertain.

What's left of Sautelle's elephants may still be at rest in Homer. The Elephant Encyclopedia reports, "According to local lore, some were buried in the field...once known as Contento's junkyard."

Despite its dilapidated state, the house still makes heads turn.

TOO COOL FOR SCHOOL

Are they really making movies in Syracuse?

In the middle of a quiet tree-lined neighborhood in Liverpool, American High is a Central New York dream factory. The 100,000 square foot space is a production company and film studio with interchangeable high school sets, office spaces, and sound stages. Inside is a hospital wing, classrooms, gymnasiums, cafeterias, and auditoriums, plus parking for trucks and storage for gear.

In August 2017, screenwriter, producer, and director Jeremy Garelick (*The Break Up*, *The Hangover*, *The Wedding Ringer*) bought the old A.V. Zogg middle school for $1 million. He'd been looking to purchase a high school in which smaller-budget genre films—young adult titles and romantic comedies—could be made affordably. There, filmmakers could craft high school movies like those from the 1980s scripted by John Hughes and Cameron Crowe and, more recently, *American Pie*, *Mean Girls*, and *Superbad*.

The actors in these films—budgeted at $7–$9 million—aren't household names, but they're familiar. Along with the production crews, they're bringing more than glamour to town. Syracuse film commissioner Eric Vinal says they hire local crew members and spend money on meals and hotel stays. He estimates that every film shot here leaves 70 percent of its budget in the area.

Each film hires 10 students from local colleges such as Syracuse University (SU), Onondaga Community College, Le Moyne, and Ithaca. Before American High, they had to leave for New York or Los Angeles for professional experience. As SU graduate and costumer Celine Rahman told the *New York Times*, "there's a place to make movies here and it's sustainable."

In May 2019, American High signed an eight-picture, first-look deal with Hulu. You can see three of them on the streaming platform: *The Binge, The Ultimate Playlist of Noise*, and *It's a Wonderful Binge.*

AMERICAN HIGH

WHAT: A film studio and production company

WHERE: 800 4th Street, Liverpool

COST: Free to drive by

PRO TIP: Watch American High's films on Hulu, and you'll see familiar Syracuse locales in a new light.

In 2021, a *New York Times* profile contained a backhanded compliment. Instead of a "high-stress production environment," American High has "the feel of a well-run summer camp."

HOW SWEET IT WAS

What town was Central New York's Candyland?

Jim Farfaglia remembers that once upon a time, his hometown smelled delicious. "If you drove . . . you used to roll your windows down when coming through Fulton . . . to smell that chocolate." From 1902 to 2003—one sweet century—Fulton was the factory town of Swiss-based Nestlé, where, in the best of times, employment swelled to 1,700. The *New York Times* cited Fulton as "the birthplace of Nestlé's Quik, the home of the Crunch Bar, the maker of mountains of morsels for chocolate-chip cookies."

A writer, local historian, and lifelong resident, Farfaglia recalled the factory closing in 2003. He later told the *Fulton Valley News* that when he saw the buildings being torn down, "It really hit me . . . what's the history among all that debris?" Though neither he nor any of his relatives worked there, Farfaglia felt compelled to write *Nestlé in Fulton, New York: How Sweet It Was*, concentrating on the everyday employees—line workers, wrappers, maintenance staff—and interviewing about 60 people for the book. Through their memories and anecdotes, he recreated what it was like to work at Nestlé: "the sights, the smells, and the taste . . . not just a description of how chocolate is made . . . [but] people . . . walking us through it."

FULTON'S CHOCOLATE PAST

WHAT: Nestlé and the Chocolate Factory

WHERE: Revisit chocolate-making at the J. W. Pratt House Museum, 177 South First Street, Fulton

COST: Donations appreciated

PRO TIP: You don't have to be a Central New York resident to enjoy *Nestlé in Fulton, New York: How Sweet It Was* by Jim Farfaglia—just a chocolate lover.

Chocolate-making wasn't the original purpose of the Fulton factory. Founder Henri Nestlé was a Swiss pharmacist who'd invented an infant formula so successful in Europe that he

The factory and town in the heyday of chocolate production. Courtesy of Jim Farfaglia.

wanted to start manufacturing in America. Nestlé originally chose Fulton as a milk-processing site: "They were looking for dairy country, dairy farm area. The river, the Erie Canal, the railroad system [were] already in place. We already had industry in Fulton." Serendipitously, back home, Henri Nestlé's Swiss neighbor had invented a milk chocolate product and wanted to expand to the US. Nestlé had an idea that launched years of milk chocolate innovation, most notably in 1938: the year that Nestlé's Crunch was born, selling for just five cents.

> At one time, Jim Farfaglia says, Fulton had "the largest chocolate-making factory in North America . . . It was the largest Nestlé factory for decades all over the world."

THE (HAIRY) EAGLE HAS LANDED

What are Honest Abe's tresses doing here in Syracuse?

Next time you get a haircut or trim, don't let those pieces fall to the floor. Save them in case you run for President. A strange historic artifact nicknamed *The Hairy Eagle* is proof that audiences will pay good money to see peculiar things, including Abraham Lincoln's locks fashioned into art most fowl.

In April 1864, an exposition called the Metropolitan Sanitary Fair was held in New York City to benefit the US Sanitary Commission, which supported sick and wounded army soldiers. Buzz surrounded one unique display under glass: an eagle perched on a globe atop a floral wreath.

In a *New York Herald* item highlighting "the curiosities in the Fair . . . [*The Hairy Eagle*] is . . . entitled to take the highest flight." Designed and donated by Mrs. Louisa Wright, wife of a former Indiana governor, the eagle "measures about twelve inches in length . . . the head, eyes, and backbone . . . formed of hair from the head of President Lincoln." The wing feathers "are made of hair from the heads of thirty-four prominent Senators, arranged in the order of their age." A wreath "of the hair of the wives of representative men" ensured women were included.

Wright commissioned Brooklyn jewelers Spies & Champney to execute her design. According to *The History Blog*, "The letter Spies & Champney sent to President Lincoln in January 1864

First Lady Mary Todd Lincoln's hair is included along with strands of members of Lincoln's Cabinet. Notable among them is Auburn son William Henry Seward, Secretary of State under Lincoln.

Yes, those feathers are all human hair. Used with permission of the Onondaga Historical Assocation.

soliciting 'as large a lock as you can well spare' is in the Library of Congress."

Afterwards, *The Hairy Eagle* became a Champney family heirloom, accompanying Mrs. Ida Champney to Syracuse when she moved in with her daughter. Donated to the Onondaga Historical Association sometime before 1917, it now rests in the OHA archives in a dim back room protected from natural light.

LINCOLN'S HAIR ART

WHAT: A human hair sculpture containing Lincoln's locks

WHERE: In storage at the Onondaga Historical Association

COST: $3 suggested donation

PRO TIP: Become a member of the OHA, and you'll have access to the Research Center. Though there's no guarantee you'll see *The Hairy Eagle*, your support will help maintain its safe storage.

THE ORIGINAL IRON MAN

What ever happened to the tin man that used to be on Geddes Street?

Millions only know the fictional Tin Man played by Jack Haley in *The Wizard of Oz* and have never seen one in real life. But in Syracuse, for most of the 20th century, the Heaphy Tin Man was an urban landmark. He stood watch over Geddes Street where locals either took him for granted or were terrified by him. By the time Ellen B. Edgerton posted online in 1998, "You've lived in Syracuse long enough when . . . the *Heaphy Tin Man* no longer scares you," he'd finally gotten off the streets, enshrined in dignity and safety in his new museum home.

Today he'd be a brand mascot, but in 1892 when D. J. Heaphy opened his shop by the Erie Canal to make wagon mud flaps, there was no such thing. According to American folklorist Archie Green, after Heaphy and Son moved to 133 North Geddes Street, "[A] worker—perhaps Charles Penfield—made a six-foot-tall tin man that had a spinner-ventilator head and placed it in front of the new shop." A surviving picture postcard (circa 1909) "represents the earliest photograph of a tin man . . . the only one that . . . can be traced to the first decade of the twentieth century."

When Heaphy opened a wholesale hardware store at Richmond Avenue and Geddes Street around 1946, tinsmith Jim Gallagher fashioned a second cowboy-hatted *Tin Man* who later made it into a 1996 Everson Museum folk-art exhibit.

HEAPHY TIN MAN

WHAT: A local landmark that terrified children

WHERE: Formerly at 133 North Geddes Street

COST: Admission fee at his new home

PRO TIP: Now inside the Onondaga Historical Association, 321 Montgomery Street

In the mid-1960s, a car took out the ventilator-headed *Tin Man* and a new one was fabricated, similar-looking but stronger, reinforced with cast-iron sewer pipes and set in concrete. A car mowed him down in 1984. When company president James Heaphy died in 1997, the last *Tin Man* was given to the Onondaga Historical Association in his memory.

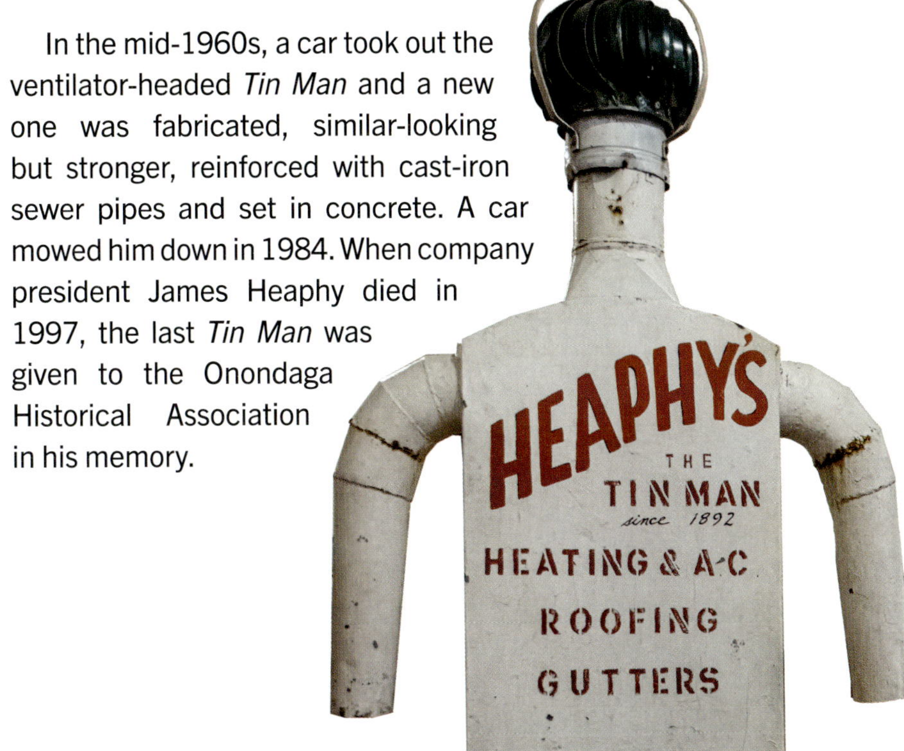

Over the decades, the stuff of many a local child's nightmares. Used with permission from the Onondaga Historical Association

---

The Heaphy Tin Man was often the victim of vandalism, his ventilator head a favorite target. Each time, he was faithfully repaired—and the statue was repainted every two years.

MINETTO'S MIDNIGHT GHOSTS

What's fact and what's fiction surrounding Gray Road?

All the stories start the same: "There are only two houses on Gray Road and a set of train tracks."

While train tracks are visible on aerial maps—and two rusted railroad signals still stand—the tracks no longer cross the road. Plus, Google Maps shows more than two houses along its length. Still, the sentence "There are twice as many ghost stories about Gray Road as there are houses" has a nice ring. And Gray Road is 1.3 miles long. Coincidence?

In the Syracuse *Post-Standard*'s now defunct Strange CNY column, a reader claimed that the house at the east end "has a dozen lit candles in the window every season." Reporter Nicole Hube of the Oswego *Palladium Times* stated that those candles "allegedly . . . commemorate the lives of 12 nuns murdered many decades ago in a serial murder spree, however I could not find any record of such event."

What Hube can confirm is that "in early November of 1926, Ethel Guinup, born approximately 1905" took her own life "by hanging herself in a barn located in the woods." She also reported that in August 1961, cabdriver Frank F. Coolidge was murdered on Gray Road by passenger Garry Rhinehart, who couldn't pay the fare. "When he called me a name I emptied the gun into the back of his head," the killer told police. Apparently, the taxi meter was still ticking away when police seized the vehicle, its instrument panel and front seat splattered with blood.

Park your car on the train tracks at midnight, and allegedly a woman in white, the murdered cabbie, or the schoolchildren will appear. Thankfully the nuns rest in peace.

Even in daylight, Gray Road feels desolate and unsettling.

Gray Road's biggest urban legend involves a group of schoolchildren. Huber wrote they were killed "when the wagon they were riding in got stuck on the Gray Road train tracks, colliding with an incoming locomotive." While no reports of the accident exist, that's the story that prompts the biggest shivers.

DARK GRAY ROAD

WHAT: A 1.3-mile road in Oswego County

WHERE: Between County Route 24 and NY-48, Minetto

COST: Free

PRO TIP: Since the train tracks no longer cross the road, there are no guarantees. Much of the land is private property, so be respectful—avoid trespassing.

A PLATFORM FOR COMMUTER ART

Why are there statues standing by 690 westbound?

Lawrence Epolito was 12 years old when he first stepped onto a train platform. He remembers thinking that the first train—its rumble, its roar, its earth-shaking power—"was like a spaceship coming in." The feeling never left him, and 30 years later, he broke the law to gift Syracuse with his tribute to train travel.

By 1982, he had become Duke Epolito, a local artist whose work had already been seen around the city. His friend Larry Zankowski suggested creating figures for the abandoned New York Central Railroad platform. Originally, seven statues were fashioned out of paper mâché and clothing; they were painted white and then coated with polyurethane for protection. The two men illegally snuck the figures onto the platform at night, just feet away from the busy traffic-filled lanes of I-690 westbound. The next day, as thousands of commuters caught their first glimpse of the spectral figures, the installation titled *Waiting for the Night Train* was an instant hit.

But over time, decay of the building, the covered platform, and vandalism left their mark on the figures Epolito regards as "a kind of graffiti" and

DUKE EPOLITO'S *NIGHT TRAIN* SCULPTURES

WHAT: Ghostly white figures wait for a train that never comes

WHERE: The New York Central Railroad platform on 1-690 W just before Exit 13

COST: Free but don't stop — it's an interstate

PRO TIP: If you want a better look, try Google Maps Street View, but a white Honda Pilot SUV and its rooftop kayak blocks the figures.

"commuter art." At least once a year, he'd jump a wall and climb onto the platform to maintain them. Now down to six, they've been remade in fiberglass. Also redone to the tune of $1.4 million was the once-crumbling platform, thanks to a NYS Department of Transportation renovation plan. Removed during the construction phase, in November 2016, the statues were returned to the new platform by DOT workers and Epolito who said, "They are part of us, they are part of me and I'm just happy and speechless that they are back."

Two of the iconic figures waiting for a train that will never come.

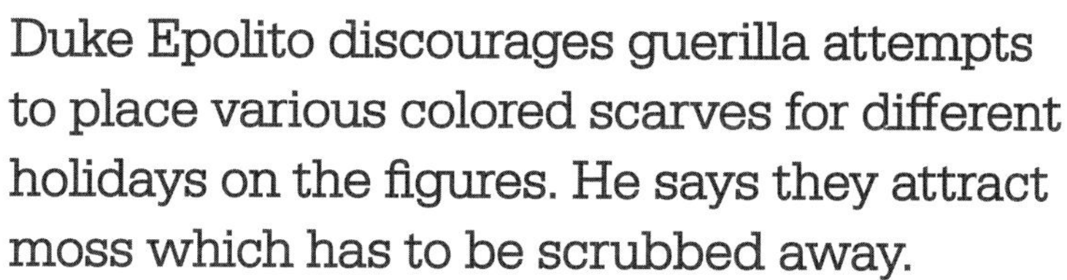

Duke Epolito discourages guerilla attempts to place various colored scarves for different holidays on the figures. He says they attract moss which has to be scrubbed away.

THE VILLAGE THAT RAISED A PRESIDENT

Where did Grover Cleveland spend his childhood?

When the boy who would be president of the United States came to Fayetteville, he had a name different from the one we know him by today.

Stephen Grover Cleveland was born in Caldwell, New Jersey, in 1837, and moved to Fayetteville in 1841 when his father, a Presbyterian minister, took a clergy position for a salary of $500. As the fifth of nine children, Cleveland grew up in a strict home where money was scarce and daily worship and Bible readings were the rule. He preferred being outdoors, fishing and swimming in Limestone Creek.

He attended grammar school at Fayetteville Academy and was described as "chuck full of fun." As for his studies, he was seen as a hardworking but not particularly bright student. At age 13, Cleveland was apprenticed to local storekeeper John McVicar, receiving a dollar a week payment plus room and board—$50 total for the year. He was diligent at his chores, honest at bookkeeping, and was promised that his salary would double his second year. To his regret, he had to leave when his father moved the family to Clinton, New York, in 1850 for a better-paying position.

In 1887, President Grover Cleveland returned to his boyhood home in Fayetteville and fondly recalled his childhood. Addressing a crowd of a thousand spectators, he said, "I find myself in a place above all others dear to me at the present time . . . It was here that

---

The historic Fayetteville home he lived in went on the market in June 2022. Listed at $320,000 for 1,576 square feet, it sold for $265,000 in August of that year.

Quiet Fayetteville's big claim to fame.

I enjoyed every pleasure, sport, and pastime of boyhood." He also referenced his boyhood love of fishing, recalling "Green Lake and the fish that I tried to catch and never caught and which I suppose are there today."

GROVER CLEVELAND'S CHILDHOOD HOME

WHAT: A three-bedroom, two-bath Colonial house that still looks the same

WHERE: 109 Academy Street, Fayetteville

COST: Free to view from the sidewalk

PRO TIP: Nearby is the home of suffragist Matilda Joslyn Gage—her son-in-law L. Frank Baum wrote *The Wonderful Wizard of Oz*. That house is open to the public, but with limited hours.

THE FALLS GUY

How did five private waterfalls become CNY's latest public-use areas?

Remember the R&B girl group TLC and their big hit "Waterfalls" from 1995? Clearly, retired Syracuse University professor Harold Jones doesn't. That song's famous refrain, "Don't go chasin' waterfalls," is the exact opposite of what he's done over the past few years. A Manlius resident, Jones has sunk $1.5 million into chasing waterfalls, but it's money well spent. Thanks to him, Central New York has two new places to enjoy with five gorgeous waterfalls between them.

Jones's first waterfall purchase was privately owned Three Falls Woods in Manlius, off Sweet Road and East Seneca Turnpike. Long known to locals who willfully ignored No Trespassing signs, the falls are in a deep ravine—part of the Onondaga Escarpment—carved by two tributaries of Limestone Creek. Described as "tiered cascaded falls," they include Staircase Falls, Tall Twins, and Cascade Falls, and have straight drops of 20 feet with tumbling water another 30-40 feet. After purchasing 80 acres, Jones donated it to the CNY Land Trust, which did some trail improvement and created a small parking lot just off Sweet Road. "I bought all the best parts of the property," he told the *Syracuse Post-Standard*, "the three small, but absolutely beautiful waterfalls, with a large ravine and lots of old-growth forest."

HAROLD JONES'S WATERFALL PHILANTHROPY

WHAT: Stunning waterfalls for everyone to enjoy

WHERE: Three Falls Woods, 4618 Sweet Road, Manlius, and Delphi Falls County Park, 2006

COST: Free but limited parking at Three Falls Woods

PRO TIP: Three Falls Woods is not advised for those with mobility issues. Delphi Falls, however, is a short distance from the parking lot along a handicapped-accessible path.

Delphi Falls in winter.

He did it again when 60 acres—including two tiered waterfalls—at Delphi Falls in Madison County came on the market. He and the property owner, real estate agents, and Madison County struck a deal: as reported by the *Post-Standard*, Jones had to "come up with $750,000 of the purchase price, which was $900,000, while Madison County funded the rest, $150,000." He donated that land as well, and today Madison County's newest park, Delphi Falls, is open to the public.

Why be the Fall guy? Jones explains, "It just gives me a very good feeling . . . allowing the community to refresh themselves by seeing these beautiful waterfalls and having contact with nature."

UP ON THE ROOF

Does someone live in the little house on that building by I-81?

Everyone loves a good mystery, especially when it's a familiar thing seen in an unexpected context. For over a century, many have wondered, "What's a nice house like you doing in a place like this?" The "nice house" was a quaint two-story Victorian, red with white trim and a white roof; the "place like this" was atop a forlorn five-story building at the corner of Wolf and Park Streets, its bricked-up windows overlooking nearby I-81.

In 2013, Gizmodo included it in a "Strange and Gorgeous Houses Built on Rooftops" roundup. In 2022, Milford, PA, visitor Misty Albaugh posted at RoadsideAmerica.com, "This wasn't something I planned to stop for, but we saw it a few times during our evening in Syracuse. It made us laugh every time, and was visible from the highway."

Even the *New York Post* wrote about it: "The mysterious house, an unofficial Syracuse landmark, has been the subject of local lore for years. One legend claimed it belonged to a woman whose house was replaced by the factory. . . . As part of that deal, the story goes, she had the home rebuilt on the roof so she could continue living there. Another rumor is that it belonged to the owner of the factory . . . so he could keep a very close eye on business."

In 2013, Syracuse *Post-Standard* reporter Rick Moriarty put those rumors to rest: "[C]omplete with a door and multiple windows [the house] is just a shell of a building to protect the

---

The architectural gimmick was meant to draw attention to the building, and it worked. A succession of owners maintained the mystery, discouraging outside visitors and photographers.

Currently under renovation, the proposed plans promise new life for the building and its rooftop house.

motor that powers the five-story building's ancient, but still working, freight elevator." He added, "Most Syracusans have no idea the complex was once a place where carriages and automobiles, power tools and mattresses were made. They just know it as 'the building with a house on the roof.'"

HOUSE ON THE ROOF AT PENFIELD MANUFACTURING

WHAT: A mysterious house atop a five-story building

WHERE: Corner of Wolf and Park Streets

COST: Free to view from the outside at street or interstate level

PRO TIP: The house is undergoing renovation, and the new color scheme is gray with white trim.

"COTTEN PICKING" IN SYRACUSE

What folk musician saw late-in-life success playing into her 80s?

When Syracuse's Reverend Larry Ellis was little, he wondered why "Old Jesus" would visit his grandma's house so often. Only later did he realize to whom he'd given the blasphemous nickname—Jerry Garcia of The Grateful Dead. Along with his band, whenever Garcia was in Syracuse, he'd come to pay tribute to Larry's grandmother, folk music legend Libba (Elizabeth) Cotten.

Cotten strummed for John F. Kennedy and wrote "Freight Train," her most famous song, at age 11. She inspired Bob Dylan and Peter, Paul, and Mary; recorded her first album at 62; appeared in a book alongside Rosa Parks and Oprah Winfrey on Black women who changed America; won a Grammy when she turned 90; and was recognized as a "living treasure" by the Smithsonian.

Cotten was self-taught on guitar and banjo. She developed

LIBBA COTTEN

WHAT: A leading figure in American folk and blues music

WHERE: Libba Cotten Grove, South State and Castle Streets

COST: Free

PRO TIP: Watch Cotten online—Smithsonian Folkways Recordings has a 1957 home movie of Cotten performing "Freight Train" at the Seeger family home.

A portrait of Libba Cotten hangs in City Hall. Her old Martin guitar is at the Onondaga Historical Association, and there's a Libba Cotten exhibit at the Erie Canal Museum.

Bronze statue by fine art sculptor Sharon BuMann.

her unique style because the banjo she used belonged to her brother, and since she couldn't change the strings, she flipped it upside down to play. Married at 15, she stopped playing because her church discouraged "worldly" pursuits. Decades later, she started working for the Seeger family, well-known for their musicianship, where her talent was rediscovered.

She recorded albums, played live concerts, and performed at the Newport Folk Festival and the Smithsonian Festival of American Folklife. In the midst of her fame in 1978, Cotten moved from Washington DC to Syracuse. She continued to record and tour, coming back to a two-story white shingle house on West Ostrander Avenue in her adopted hometown.

Though she passed away in 1987 at age 95, recognition continued to come her way. In 2012, a bronze sculpture was unveiled at Libba Cotten Grove on Castle Street, and she was inducted into the Rock and Roll Hall of Fame in 2022.

THAT SEVENTIES MALL

How did memories of PennCan launch Syracuse Nostalgia?

A name that was proposed for I-81—but never agreed upon—was the name developers chose when a new shopping mall opened March 25, 1976. PennCan Mall's advertising introduced itself with a map indicating "HERE WE ARE!" at "the intersection of Routes 81 (the PennCan Highway) and 481. . . . Easy to reach, easy to like!"

Along with its location, the mall promoted "The Story of the PennCan Clock," built in Boston 100 years ago; shipped to Tacoma, Washington, where it became a popular landmark; and then brought to Central New York. The promotion went, "This is now the PennCan Clock, the focal point of our great Central Court . . . this great timepiece, destined soon to become the meeting place of Central New York. 'Let's Meet at The Clock!'"

While the mall was built to accommodate four department stores and 80 other stores, it opened with fewer than half that number. Articles dated March 25 described occupancy as "30-plus" stores, with opening ceremonies held in the center court. Stores would come and go from the original structure, and additions would be built, but the idea of meeting at the clock took hold, especially with teenagers. A March 1988 article, "Mall Rats Bring Thefts, Fights, and Drugs," singled out teens visiting the mall. "At [PennCan], shoplifting is a larger problem," one store owner said. "They'll steal your eye teeth if you don't watch them."

The Center Court Clock still stands, now inside Driver's Village after auto dealer Roger Burdick bought the abandoned PennCan Mall in 2000 and repurposed it into an auto mall.

Brian Hamilton of SyracuseNostalgia.com checks his watch under the unmistakable profile of the PennCan clock. Courtesy of SyracuseNostalgia.com.

Yet today, with area malls shuttered or in jeopardy, it's a former mall rat who's behind SyracuseNostalgia.com. Brian Hamilton's love for PennCan Mall led him to collect photos, articles, advertising, and other memorabilia and share it online. The response was so overwhelmingly positive, it led to a new, more expansive multimedia website packed with tidbits of Syracuse's past.

PENNCAN, THE CLOCK, AND SYRACUSE NOSTALGIA

WHAT: A mall's glory days brings back memories

WHERE: 5885 Circle Drive East, Cicero

COST: Free to visit the showroom and see the clock

PRO TIP: Visit SyracuseNostalgia.com to read more about PennCan mall and other lost-to-time places, people, and events.

STORM OF THE CENTURY

What was Syracuse's worst snowstorm?

In 1993, March—a month that typically "comes in like a lion and goes out like a lamb"—delivered the tyrannosaurus rex of snowstorms to the entire Northeast, with Central New York caught in the middle.

Luckily, Syracuse had plenty of warning starting on Friday, March 12, with a sound everyone recognized: the electronic drone of the Emergency Broadcast System alert as radios and televisions across New York blared the first-ever statewide activation.

The National Weather Service in Philadelphia had identified a weather event they were calling "the Storm of the Century." Blizzard warnings from West Virginia to Maine were issued.

Syracusans smartly stocked up on food and entertainment. One Wegmans supermarket did three days' worth of business the day before the storm. Milk buyers at Byrne Dairy formed lines that ran the length of the building. A Fairmount video store (remember those?) reported that 500 people rented movies, some taking as many as seven at a time.

Fortunately, the storm hit on a Saturday and Sunday. The entire state was paralyzed, with the NYS Thruway completely closed. In Syracuse, Centro buses shut down, all flights at Hancock Airport were cancelled, and stranded business travelers filled all 444

THE BLIZZARD OF 1993

WHAT: A March 13-14 storm that broke multiple records in Syracuse

WHERE: All across Central New York

COST: Free to revisit in memory

PRO TIP: Although it doesn't cover the Blizzard of '93, Jim Farfaglia's *Snowstorms of Central New York* digs deep into the Blizzard of '66, which some claim was much worse.

Top left courtesy of Mary Salibrici. Bottom left and above right courtesy of Mary Guialtieri.

rooms at what was then the Hotels at Syracuse Square. Snowplows stopped venturing out after 7 p.m. Saturday because conditions were so bad.

The Syracuse *Post-Standard* noted that during the worst of the storm, "snow fell at a rate of nearly 4 inches per hour at one point and winds blew up to 46 mph." Over the weekend of March 13-14, the two-day Snowmaggedon dumped 42.9 inches on Syracuse. CNYCentral.com reports, "It was the most snow in a 24-hour period . . . and helped set a record for most snowfall of the season in Syracuse at 192.1 inches."

According to syracuse.com, "The roof caved in at the PennCan Mall, and the roof of the Carrier Dome was deflated . . . to protect it from the weight of the snow."

CLARISSA EXPLAINS IT ALL

Is the Landmark Theatre haunted?

The most famous ghost in Syracuse—the Landmark Theatre ghost—can't exactly speak up for herself. So certain details remain in dispute. What's widely accepted is that her name is Clarissa, she wears a white dress, and she's typically seen in the balcony or on the stairs. Often the smell of lilacs accompanies her. An aspiring actress, she was somehow connected to the Landmark when she died.

A detailed variation claims she was in love with a theater electrician whom she saw electrocuted onstage; in rushing to save him, she fell from the balcony to her death.

Though he's never glimpsed her, Bill Knowlton—a longtime Syracuse radio personality and the theater's resident historian—was the first person to go public about her initial sighting in the 1970s. In 2022, Knowlton clarified her origin story: "As a charter member of the Landmark Board I was the one to 'discover' who we thought was 'Claire.' She was seen by several stagehands who were cleaning up the theatre . . . by the top of the balcony by the exit."

In a 2010 interview, Knowlton placed the sighting around 2 or 3 a.m. with the workers yelling, "Lady, can we help you? You're not supposed to be here.'" He said they were "big, burly men who didn't necessarily believe in ghosts," but afterwards "they would refuse to talk about it." During a ghost-hunting investigation, "Claire" communicated that her name was

---

The story of the Landmark Theatre's Clarissa inspired Syracuse-based children's book author Bruce Coville to write *The Ghost in the Third Row.*

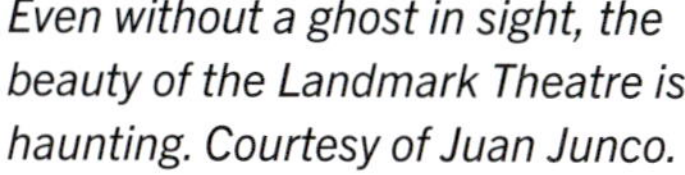

Even without a ghost in sight, the beauty of the Landmark Theatre is haunting. Courtesy of Juan Junco.

THE LANDMARK THEATRE GHOST

WHAT: A spectral woman in white who prefers the balcony seats

WHERE: 362 South Salina Street

COST: Admission prices vary

PRO TIP: Keep your eyes and ears open for another ghost—a night watchman with his dog who's been seen and/or heard in the theater.

Clarissa. Most recently, Knowlton wrote, "My story is that Clarissa or her husband were on the staff of Loew's and that she was a frustrated actress who decided to inhabit the theatre after she died. Nowhere did I hear of any falling off the balcony."

It's also said that Clarissa hates cigarettes, but smoking in the theater is illegal, ghost or no ghost.

RETAIL MAKE-BELIEVE

What was that fairytale building near I-81?

In the late 1980s, if you couldn't afford a trip to Disneyworld, you went to Switz's. Whoever wrote the 1985 TV commercial jingle "Get away . . . take a Switz's holiday!" understood the magic of that one-of-a-kind store. For a handful of years, Switz's wowed Central New York with elaborate seasonal displays in which animatronic human figures, animals, and monstrous creatures came to life, delighting adults and terrifying children.

The successful variety store, founded by Mark Switz in 1954, relocated from a shopping plaza to a new store across the street in 1984. Though the distance was short, the move was bold; Switz's spent $3 million on a fairytale structure unlike anything in the area. The new store was a massive Swiss chalet on steroids, its three-story Bavarian 'Old World' exterior rising to a 71-foot-tall peaked clock tower. Writer Cortney Pitcher in her Mattydale Memories newspaper column wrote, "Why a clock tower for a

SWITZ'S

WHAT: A landmark Swiss chalet-style building that once sold craft and seasonal items

WHERE: 5404 South Bay Road, Salina

COST: Free to view from the parking lot

PRO TIP: Most recently, it was world headquarters of tech company CXTec, but the building's gray and blue corporate makeover can't hide its unique silhouette.

With 2,500 square feet reserved for seasonal displays, Switz's magical, elaborately conceived, holiday-themed settings, particularly during Halloween and Christmas, attracted families and even lured tour buses to the store.

Switz's distinctive clock tower. Courtesy of SyracuseNostalgia.com.

variety store? Interstate 81 drivers could see the clock as they passed by." Just to set it in place, it "took a 110-foot crane boom to lift the gigantic clockwork to the tiptop."

Inside, the store was even more staggering: 40,000 square feet on the main floor and another 20,000 square feet in the basement for storage. A little red schoolhouse promoted back-to-school items, and an elaborate Christmas setting included animatronic humans and animals—half a dozen singing carolers, toys and woodland creatures, and Santa Claus—amidst revolving Christmas trees, fully decorated with twinkling lights.

Halloween, however, solidified Switz's position as every child's favorite store. Yet in the early 1990s, arts and crafts chain stores entered the Syracuse market, hurting local retailers. So when Switz's announced it was closing nine years after its stunning relocation, customers like Christine Zender—who'd always picked out Halloween costumes there—were shocked: "It seems unreal that Switz's would close. It's an institution."

The building today.

LOVABLE LORD OF DARKNESS

What ever happened to Oscar?

You can tell the adults who spent their childhood in Syracuse by their reaction to three words: *Halloween at Switz's*. From 1984 to 1993, every kid in Central New York passed through the variety store's doors to pick out their Halloween costume and to see Oscar.

A mechanical monster, Oscar was—at 14 feet and 1,700 pounds—a giant ogre with the horrific honorific Lord of Darkness. He was the centerpiece of Switz's new store on South Bay Road, and his otherworldly presence inside lived up to the store's fairytale-inspired exterior.

Oscar was brought to Syracuse by Switz's president Bertel Schmidt. After attending an international toy fair in West Germany, Schmidt came back with two animatronic displays. One was a five-piece Skeleton Band. Bony musicians played bass, guitar, drums, violin, and horn, dressed in pirate, clown, Davy Crockett, and other Halloween costumes.

But the second one, Oscar, was the big hit. Syracuse *Post-Standard* reporter Johnathan Croyle wrote, "There were only two of them in the world and Bert Schmidt bought one, hoping that the giant monster would fit inside his new store." It barely did. The hulking, saber-toothed, green-haired creature's allure was that he was scary, but not too scary. As Croyle tells it, "Oscar towered over customers in a huge display in the front of the

SWITZ'S OSCAR THE OGRE

WHAT: A giant animatronic Halloween monster

WHERE: Online at SyracuseNostalgia.com

COST: Free

PRO TIP: Oscar logo merchandise is available at SyracuseNostalgia.com

Oscar and the boys in the band. Courtesy of SyracuseNostalgia.com.

store, bellowing and swaying over wide-eyed children. He carried a giant wooden club in his right hand and was decorated with 'severed heads' chained to his clothing."

Oscar became the focus of Switz's yearly Halloween promotions and its annual coloring contest. Because of him, Switz's busiest day was the Saturday before Halloween. But hard times fell on Switz's due to the shifting retail landscape, and the store closed in 1993. Yet those who've met Oscar still smile at his memory: those were the days.

Switz's originally paid $23,000 for Oscar, but in 1993 Richard Wagoner of Cicero bought him for $7,000. Oscar was later auctioned off for $2,000. Today, his whereabouts are unknown.

A SUCKER BORN EVERY MINUTE

Why did the public fall for the Cardiff Giant?

Its materials came from Idaho, its manufacture took place in Chicago, and it was buried under the roots of a tree on a farm outside Syracuse. When it came to light, it was first celebrated as "the new wonder" and later pronounced a fake. The Cardiff Giant remains one of the most elaborate hoaxes of all time.

In 1868, atheist George Hull spent $2,600—roughly $56,740 today—to win an argument over a Bible verse that stated "there were giants in the earth in those days." Hull planned a long con, buying land in Fort Dodge, Iowa, to obtain a 12' x 4' x 2' block of gypsum. Shipped to Chicago, it was shaped by a stonecutter into the likeness of a man, then in Cardiff, New York, it was buried on the property of Hull's cousin William Newell.

A year later, Newell hired two men to dig a well at that spot, unearthing the figure in October 1869. According to History.com, "Since Cardiff was already known for its fossil deposits, many surmised that the body was an ancient man . . . petrified by the waters of a nearby swamp." The 10-foot, nearly 3,000-pound figure was hailed by the *Syracuse Daily Standard* as "A NEW WONDER." A group of businessmen headed by Cortland resident David Hannum bought the Cardiff Giant, brought it to Syracuse, and then took it on tour.

When P. T. Barnum offered $50,000 for the giant and was refused, he had one made and advertised it as the real one. David Hannum derisively said about those paying to see Barnum's fake, "There's a sucker born every minute," a quote

---

Hull's resourceful cousin charged admission, and in the first week alone, 2,500 gawkers paid Newell 50 cents apiece to see the Cardiff Giant.

Immortalizing the stone-cold scam that hoodwinked thousands.

later misattributed to Barnum himself. By 1870, both giants were recognized as fakes, yet they still showed up now and then for public display. Today, the Cardiff Giant is at the Farmer's Museum in Cooperstown, NY.

THE CARDIFF GIANT

WHAT: A fake-news stone man

WHERE: A historical marker at Tully Farms Road (County Road 234) 0.1 miles north of Webster Road, Cardiff

COST: Free

PRO TIP: There are actually two historical markers, one at the address above, and the other at the intersection of Cherry Valley Turnpike (US 20) and Field Lane.

(ALMOST) THE WORLD'S SMALLEST CHURCH

What's that building in the middle of that pond?

It all began in the mid-1980s with a cross in the middle of the Mason family's pond in Oneida. Two passing visitors said to the pond's owner, Chandler Mason, that they admired the cross and thought it would be nice to have a church beneath it. "He always wanted to do things that were unique," his daughter Beth Mason told Iris St. Meran of Spectrum News, so he consulted a *Guinness Book of World Records* for the world's smallest church and its dimensions, and made one just a bit smaller.

He built the church in his garage. Donated rocks formed the island. To transfer the structure, he waited until winter. "We took a snowmobile and took it out across the ice," Beth explained.

Perfect for a tiny wedding, it's the size of a walk-in closet: 6 ½ by 4 ½ feet. Asked how many it holds, Beth says, "Comfortably, five people. A minister, bride, groom, and two witnesses." The floor area is 51" by 81" or 28.68 square feet—enough for a pulpit and two chairs. Befitting a church, it also has a stained-glass window. It's nondenominational and open to the public.

In 1989, Cross Island Chapel was the world's smallest church, but since then, the *Guinness Book of World Records* has verified a smaller one in Switzerland. Today, it can lay claim to being the tiniest church in America.

Though Chandler passed away in 2003 at age 67, his church endures, which is what he wanted said his widow, Kay Mason. In

CROSS ISLAND CHAPEL

WHAT: America's smallest church

WHERE: Sconondoa Road, Oneida

COST: Free to visit

PRO TIP: The chapel can be rented for weddings and special events.

Here's the church, here's the steeple . . .

a 2011 interview with the Utica *Observer-Dispatch*, she explained, "He wanted to do something to honor God. He thought that people would look at it and say, "'[S]omebody cares, God cares' . . . [W]e wanted to let people know that."

Wedding guests who can't fit inside Cross Island Chapel can stand outside on the dock, or observe from boats anchored in the pond.

THE MAGIC KEY

Wasn't there a children's TV show seen only in Syracuse?

Eat your heart out Netflix, Hulu, Max. At the dawn of network television, a pioneering group of Syracuse showrunners launched a series that continued for 6,200 episodes over 27 years. Starting in the mid-1950s, *The Magic Toy Shop* was broadcast live from the studios of WHEN-TV.

The show's main characters were Toy Shop owner Merrily, her friend Eddie Flum Num, storyteller Mr. Trolley, and Twinkle the Clown who "spoke" by playing the Magic Piano.

On the air six months before *Captain Kangaroo*, *The Magic Toy Shop* debuted on February 28, 1955, running weekdays from 9:00–9:30 a.m.

The station used in-house talent—all Syracuse University (SU) graduates: Merrily was continuity director Marylin Herr, Eddie Flum Num was station artist Socrates Sampson, Mr. Trolley was Lew O'Donnell with a PhD from SU, and Twinkle was station musician Tony Riposo. A later addition was the Play Lady, Jean Daugherty, who stepped in after Herr gave birth to her first child. Daugherty, who wrote all 6,200 episodes, had degrees in education and communications.

WHEN-TV program director Gordon Alderman noted that in the first nine years, "we only missed four programs," preempting the show for the death of JFK, space flight coverage, and Soviet leader Nikita Khrushchev's US visit.

Not everything ran smoothly. There were some who feared that Mr. Trolley would be electrocuted. His "trolleyhead" required O'Donnell to press a button to light his nose. Whenever he did, he'd get a shock.

The Toy Shop gang and the electrifying Mr. Trolley. Courtesy of Corky Herr.

In 1996, Daugherty wrote, "adults who were 'our children' . . . can still quote the opening: 'Boys and girls, this is the door to the wonderful Magic Toy Shop. But to open it you need a key.' Thousands of Central New York youngsters put their thumbs at the corners of their mouths and turned them up into a smile."

If you grew up in Syracuse, you know what that gesture meant: a smile is the magic key to the magic door to the wonderful Magic Toy Shop.

THE MAGIC TOY SHOP

WHAT: A groundbreaking local children's television show

WHERE: Broadcast from the former WHEN-TV studios

COST: Free if you can view a clip online

PRO TIP: Visit SyracuseNostalgia.com where a *The Magic Toy Shop Reunion* show hosted by TV news anchor Ron Curtis—Syracuse's Walter Cronkite—features clips of the show.

SIGNS OF THE TIMES

Who's behind those local historical markers?

Why would a guy who's building the future sink a portion of his fortune into looking back? Bill Pomeroy had already made history as the founder of CXTec and TERACAI—two successful, Syracuse-based, multimillion-dollar technology companies with global impact—when he created a foundation that literally signposts the past. His pivot followed a 2004 diagnosis of an aggressive form of leukemia that required treatment in Syracuse and Boston. A May 2005 stem cell transplant turned the page on cancer, giving him a next chapter to pursue two parallel stories: funding research and support for blood cancers, and providing grant monies to individuals and organizations celebrating their community's history.

The William G. Pomeroy Foundation is familiar to locals who've stopped to read historical markers throughout Central New York. But the Foundation's generosity has granted funding for roadside markers and plaques nationwide—more than 2,000 since 2005.

WILLIAM G. POMEROY FOUNDATION HISTORICAL MARKERS

WHAT: A millionaire tech founder preserves history through signage

WHERE: The Foundation website has a searchable historical markers map.

COST: Free

PRO TIP: At the actual sites described in many of these Secret Syracuse entries, you'll see a William G. Pomeroy Foundation marker.

In many ways, historical markers are the original selfie spots, prompting visitors to stop along roadsides, at parks and historic sites, and even back home in their own neighborhoods.

Old and new historical markers provided by the Foundation.

This is not your grandpa's staid historical marker. The Foundation's colorful signage highlights a variety of themes: local and regional food with Hungry for History, folklore with Legends & Lore, watery byways with Historic Transportation Canals, and Revolutionary War soldiers with Patriot Burials. Plus, they fill a gap few realize exists. Inclusion in the National Register of Historic Places—while a significant honor—does not include funding for signage. Neither does New York State, so the Foundation makes them possible.

Like artwork or sculpture, these markers deserve historical preservation. The Historical Marker Database includes more than 172,000, but many have not been cleaned or maintained for years. In an annual observance similar to Earth Day, the Foundation created National Historic Marker Day. The last Friday of April is a chance for individuals and communities to come together to maintain their local historical markers by cleaning them, thereby providing an opportunity to celebrate and preserve history.

THE ART OF WALKING

Are mysterious crop circles appearing in the snow?

Some people describe themselves as working artists. Laura Reeder is a *walking* artist. She interacts with the earth one step at a time, her footsteps creating a trail that becomes a drawing she calls a cultivator. She's drawn them in sand, snow, and leaves, starting six years ago on the beaches of Swampscott, Massachusetts. Now that she's back in the Syracuse area—where she lived years ago—she's found a different surface to walk on. These days, Reeder says, her winter canvas is a pristine expanse of snow: "These walks are usually anywhere from two miles to eight miles long now, and if anybody is obsessive enough to follow in the walks it's a good long hike."

Reeder has created cultivators at Woodland Reservoir, in Thornden Park, in the village of Cazenovia, and at the Oneida Community Mansion House. She's also drawn in the sand at Southwick Beach.

For the winter cultivators, she wears snowshoes. The beach cultivators began with a rake. And she continues to use a rake in her newest cultivators drawn in fallen leaves on grassy lawns. Those are smaller because all that raking can be tiring.

A drone enables her to photograph the cultivator from above, yet it's not the picture she's focused on: "I'm much more interested in the walk and the journey in the moment." The swirls, curls, and spirals are reminiscent of clouds, creating the same wonder and desire to find meaning in their shapes. Reeder admits, "People want to talk about my cultivators. Everybody's got a story: 'This reminds me of this, this reminds me of that.' So now the nice treat is when I share an image, the stories come pouring in."

Like clouds, Laura Reeder's work is fleeting. Snow melts. Leaves blow away. Sand is swept clean by the tide. That's part of the process.

Walk-in-the-park art.
Courtesy of Laura K. Reeder.

For Reeder, the most important outcome has been this "cultivating of stories. That's what emerged. Stories about what we learn from each other and from the earth."

LAURA REEDER'S CULTIVATORS

WHAT: A walking drawing in snow, leaves, or sand

WHERE: In and around locales in Central New York

COST: Free to view

PRO TIP: If you stumble across a cultivator, walk it. That's what it's there for. And don't be afraid to exit in the middle. It's not like a labyrinth—there are no rules.

GET OUT OF THE WAYSIDE

What's Syracuse's most haunted spot?

The Wayside has had different owners and gone by different names, but the one constant of this building in Elbridge has been its haunted reputation. Built in 1830 by Squire Munro, it was the Munro House when a Civil War soldier was murdered there. It burned down twice, was subsequently rebuilt, ended its life as an inn, and became a restaurant after being sold to Fred Weber in 1967. Weber has acknowledged seeing a little girl at the top of the stairs, and described his own granddaughter's encounter with "a grim, ghostly woman" she called "the lady with the funny eyes."

Mediums and psychics have visited, and countless paranormal investigations have been conducted at the Wayside since Margo Spain took over 16 years ago. All conclude there are three ghosts present: the soldier, a young child who died after

THE WAYSIDE IRISH PUB

WHAT: A haunted restaurant and bar

WHERE: 101 West Main Street, Elbridge

COST: A bit of bravery

PRO TIP: If you go for a meal or a drink, be warned: patrons and bartenders have been touched and poked by unseen presences, and cold spots have been reported.

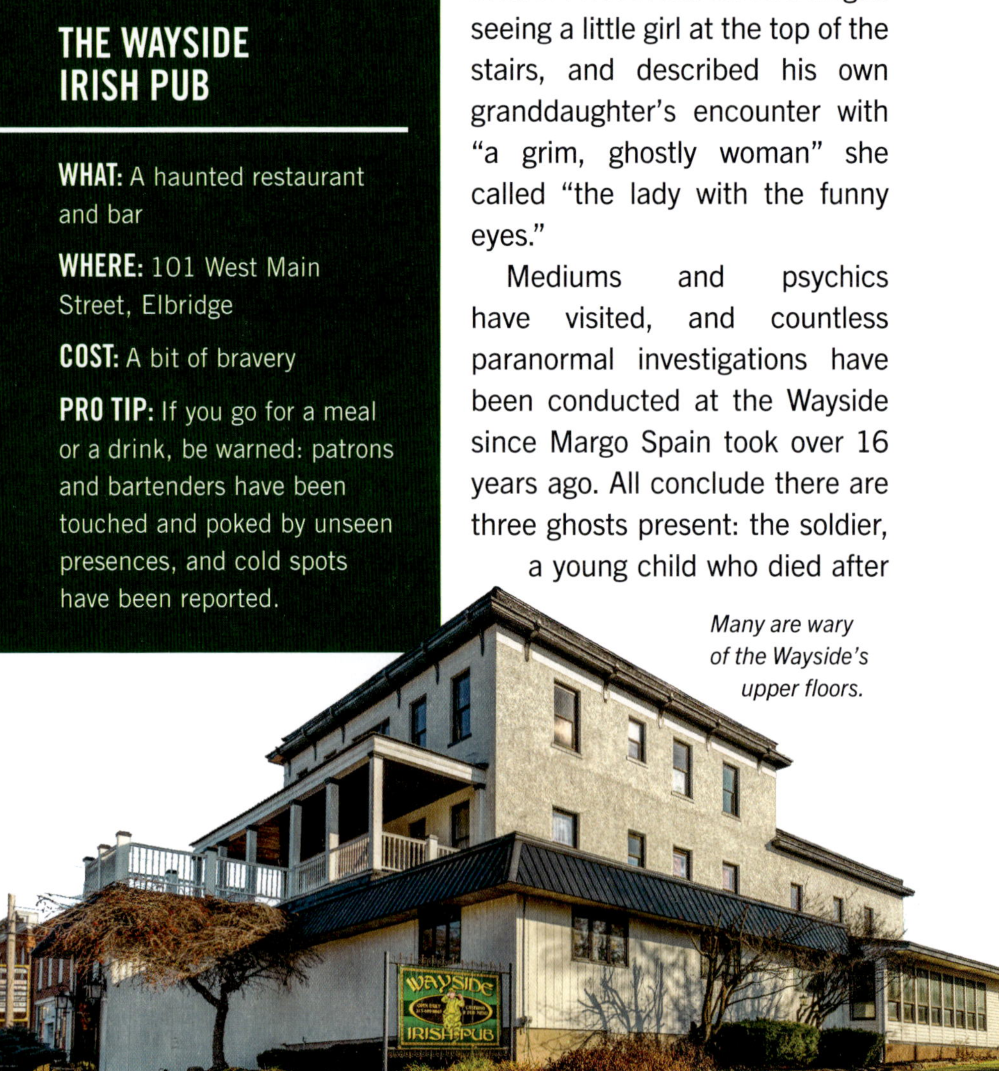

Many are wary of the Wayside's upper floors.

The bar and restaurant at ground level.

an illness, and a third entity—the most famous of all. Sarah is the Wayside's most active ghost, a young girl frequently seen on the staircase of the three-story building which keeps its upper two floors closed to the public. Sarah, it is said, took her own life, "but she does not want that story told," insists Spain. "She has tantrums after there's investigators here and they talk about it."

Mystery writer Dennis Webster and paranormal investigator Bernadette Peck of the group Ghost Seekers of Central New York wrote about the Wayside in the book *Haunted Mohawk Valley*. During the team's visit, Margo Spain was pushed from behind while on the stairs. Some saw "an ominous, full-figured shadow person." Walking and footsteps were heard coming from the empty second floor. The group concluded, "The Wayside is highly paranormal and well deserving of its reputation."

A workman hired to remodel the second floor heard creepy voices and had enough unsettling experiences that he quit on the spot.

THE HAZARDS OF A COMPANY TOWN

What process turned a quiet village into a major industry?

Syracuse stood at the crossroads of 19th-century commerce, leaving a legacy of names and terms we've all heard. But can we explain what they are? Take, for example, Solvay Process. What is it? Why does the village share the name? And which came first, village or process?

It began with soda ash, an essential raw mineral. Soda ash is used worldwide in the production of glass, detergents, soaps, chemicals, and other industrial products. Back in the 1800s, a Belgian chemist named Ernest Solvay came up with an industrial process to produce soda ash. He patented the process of producing it in large quantities and, with his brother, started a company in Belgium in 1863.

A few years later, former Syracusan William B. Cogswell was a mining engineer overseeing Mine la Motte, a lead mine in Missouri. He knew that key materials in the process—water, limestone, and salt brine—were plentiful in Syracuse. Since American industries were importing soda ash from Europe, why not make it in Syracuse? He approached the Hazard family of Rhode Island, owners of Mine la Motte, convincing Rowland Hazard II to back his venture. They obtained the American rights to the Solvay process in 1881 and built a soda ash manufacturing plant in Geddesburgh just outside Syracuse. In 1884, the Solvay Process Company opened with Hazard as president and Cogswell as vice president.

The Solvay Process Company was so influential, the village changed its name to Solvay. By 1917, it employed 7,000 workers, shaping the area for generations to come.

Solvay Process then . . .
and what's left now.

SOLVAY PROCESS COMPANY

WHAT: Soda ash production repurposes a village

WHERE: All of Solvay

COST: Free

PRO TIP: Solvay's Piercefield neighborhood still has elegant homes originally built for officers of the Solvay Process Company. Start exploring with Piercefield Drive.

All the materials were available at their fingertips: salt brine from wells in Tully, limestone from nearby Split Rock, and water from Onondaga Lake. Transportation practically came to their doorstep; both the Erie Canal and the New York Central Railroad passed through the plant.

Due in part to its success, it was absorbed by Allied Chemical in 1920. In 1985, the Solvay Process Company closed, and its extensive physical plant was demolished.

BUCKET LIST

Why did Solvay need an aerial tramway?

Remember when Governor Andrew Cuomo's 2017-18 Executive Budget included $15 million for an aerial gondola from the Fairgrounds to the Amphitheater? Few realize that Solvay once had a sky-high system of transport, and while it did involve rock, this wasn't of the musical variety.

The Solvay Process Company saw explosive growth in its early years, and horse-drawn carts carrying limestone couldn't keep up. The Split Rock Cable Road, an aerial system of transport, began operating in May 1889. In an industry journal in 1988, Mark DeLawyer described it as "essentially the industrial equivalent of a ski lift. . . . A continuous wire rope, carrying buckets, transported broken limestone . . . between the Split Rock Quarries south of Syracuse, to the main plant in the village of Solvay." Spaced 75 feet apart, the buckets traveled 250 feet a minute pulled by a 35-horsepower engine. The biggest challenge of the 3.25-mile route was Terry Road Hill until they dug through it, creating a 534-foot tunnel 10 feet high and 12 feet wide. Afterwards, the limestone-filled buckets descended on gravity alone, with the empty buckets pulled uphill, moving 5,000 buckets—5 million pounds of crushed rock—every 24 hours.

THE SKYHIGH SPLIT ROCK CABLE ROAD

WHAT: Aerial buckets carried boys and stone

WHERE: From Split Rock to the Solvay Process plant

COST: Free to look for evidence along the route

PRO TIP: The only known remains are foundations for the quarry terminal, the towers, and the Terry Hill Tunnel. However, a tower base may still be hidden in the weeds or some other overgrown spot.

A Cable Road postcard. Courtesy of Onondaga County Public Library, New York Heritage Digital Collections.

Young daredevils couldn't resist hitching a ride. DeLawyer said, "[T]he quarry patrol, company detectives, and local police couldn't keep the kids off the cable," and claimed Solvay employees weren't immune to the temptation: "How do you think mechanics got out to the quarry? How about employees who lived near the line, or down in the village? They rode the buckets! Think of it as an early attempt at mass employee transit." However, riding the buckets "was never 'officially condoned' by the company."

The Cable Road was shut down in December 1911 and dismantled after the company switched mining operations to the Jamesville Quarry.

Solvay engineer Edward Trump designed the Cable Road. Though "[n]ot a famous public figure on the order of a Ford," DeLawyer argued, "he was nevertheless one of America's greatest mechanical engineers."

FIRE IN THE HOLE

What happened at Split Rock?

When the Solvay Process Company stopped quarrying limestone at Split Rock, its affiliate company Semet-Solvay found a use for the area. Originally established to build coke ovens, Semet-Solvay had begun to manufacture munitions at Split Rock, starting with TNT production in 1915. The plant also produced picric acid, poison gas, and gunpowder for shells during World War I. Round-the-clock production was the norm for Split Rock, which produced nearly a quarter of the TNT used by American troops in artillery shells. The facility was surrounded by 14 miles of fence guarded by 300 patrolmen.

By 1918, the plant employed 3,000 people and was producing 30,000 pounds of TNT a day.

On July 2, 1918, 600 men were working the 3-11 shift. That evening, an overheated gear in a machine set off a fire in TNT Building #1 at 8:30 p.m. When the fire whistle blew, firemen rushed to control the blaze inside the 140-foot wooden structure, but once the fire burned through the roof of the building, a southerly breeze worsened the situation. The fire hoses suddenly lost pressure. Some men stayed believing that once water pressure was restored, they could put out the fire. Others ran.

The one ton of TNT inside the building ignited in a blast of searing light and a concussive roar, sending a massive fireball into the night sky where it disintegrated into falling sparks. Those nearby were catapulted into the air and landed, burnt beyond recognition. Fifty men died in the fire. Ten buildings

---

A far worse disaster was averted. If the fire had reached the 400 tons of TNT stored in a nearby area, the explosion would have destroyed the city of Syracuse.

Split Rock in better days. Courtesy of Onondaga County Public Library, New York Heritage Digital Collections.

were destroyed. The company suffered $1,000,000 in losses. A little over four months later, World War I ended, and on December 31, 1918, Split Rock closed for good.

Today, as might be expected, the abandoned area is the source of many ghost stories and alleged hauntings.

SPLIT ROCK EXPLOSION

WHAT: An uncontrolled fire devastates a munitions plant

WHERE: 3900 Onondaga Boulevard, Camillus

COST: $1 million and 50 lives

PRO TIP: If visiting an abandoned quarry isn't your thing, pay your respects at the Solvay-Semet Memorial in Section B of Oakwood Cemetery.

MAKING MARRIAGE COMPLEX

What Oneida Community practice is taboo today?

The Oneida Community was a mid-19th century Utopian community whose 300 members lived under one roof in an elegant Mansion House that still stands today. But its founder John Humphrey Noyes promoted illegal practices that today are associated with the likes of Jeffrey Epstein and R. Kelly. For the more than three decades that it lasted—1848 to 1880—even its followers were torn by these beliefs.

Born in Vermont in 1811, Noyes experienced a religious conversion in 1831, becoming a minister. He believed in the ability to become free of sin (called Christian Perfection) and formed a religious group that settled near Oneida Creek. The Oneida Community believed in complex marriage. Monogamy, Noyes argued, was impure. Group love was ideal, thus the Oneida Community lived as a communal family and practiced communal sex. Noyes oversaw the continual change of partners, with community elders initiating the youngest believers. Children reaching puberty were assigned older partners, many in their 50s and 60s. Childbearing was a community decision and involved selective breeding. Children lived separately from their parents. In his book *Without Sin: The Life and Death of*

THE ONEIDA COMMUNITY AND MANSION HOUSE

WHAT: A mid-1800s Utopian community

WHERE: 170 Kenwood Avenue, Oneida

COST: Admission fee for the museum

PRO TIP: The Mansion House is a museum, inn, and National Historic Landmark. Book a stay at the inn, and you'll receive a complimentary tour of the museum.

the Oneida Community, historian Spencer Klaw describes how a mother, left alone with her son in rare moments, asked if he loved her. "I always melted," he recalled as an adult. "I would reach up and put my arms around her neck. I remember how tightly she held me and how long, as though she would never let me go."

The Oneida Community promoted music, painting, and poetry; encouraged games and sports; regarded collaborative work as joyous; and established thriving businesses. Yet complex marriage beliefs led to threats of prosecution from outsiders. After Noyes fled to Canada in 1879, the group abandoned its religious practices and focused on its business endeavors.

Once a silverware company, Oneida began manufacturing stainless steel flatware in the 1960s. No longer owned by the Community, Oneida is now one of the world's largest tableware manufacturers.

Elegant accomodations at the Mansion House. Courtesy of Juan Junco.

THE CONEY ISLAND OF CNY

What happened to Onondaga Lake's resorts?

Let's assume happy places don't harbor ghosts since no spirits have been spotted along Onondaga Lake's West Shore Trail. But the area is haunted—by memories of its brief time as the Syracuse Riviera.

Seven postcard-perfect venues characterize the Golden Age of Onondaga Lake's Amusement Parks and Resorts from 1875 through 1920. Include the southeastern end, and the number grows to 12. There, the massive Iron Pier was The Gateway to Onondaga Lake. Advertised as "A MAGNIFICENT PAVILION 600 feet by 50 feet, Dancing Hall 90 feet by 50 feet . . . Promenade Balcony 600 feet on the lake front," the "Iron" was an exaggeration, as the pier was made of wood.

The first resort, Lakeview Point, was built in 1872; today's Lakeview Amphitheater stands there. At the Maple Bay Hotel, "the king of all summer resorts" had a beach and dance pavilion; its Rustic Theater seated 2,500 and hosted vaudeville acts. Rockaway Beach was geared to sportsmen, especially duck hunters, with a 25-cent duck dinner.

White City's famous Shoot the Chutes propelled riders in boats into a man-made lagoon. Its 25,000 electric lights illuminated a Japanese tea garden and miniature scenic railway. Pleasant Beach had a daredevil hot-air balloon act and a famous all-day clambake and was one of the last resorts standing until it was torn

---

Trolleys serviced these resorts, and while the introduction of the automobile didn't help, the real death knell was Solvay Process Company's disposal of waste along Onondaga Lake's western shore.

Two of the lake's many resorts.
Courtesy of Liverpool Public Library.

down in 1954 for I-690. On the southeastern shore, Danforth Salt Pool was a popular salt spring-fed pool with an island in the center, and at nearby Star Park, Babe Ruth played two exhibition games in August 1922.

The one resort that still exists—in name only—is Long Branch Park. Back then, it had a roller coaster and a carousel, which, years later, became the centerpiece of Carousel Mall, now Destiny USA. Today, it's part of the Onondaga County Parks system.

ONONDAGA LAKE RESORTS

WHAT: Amusement parks from 1875 to 1920

WHERE: A C-shaped stretch concentrated along the western shore

COST: Free to visit Long Branch Park

PRO TIP: Those not mentioned—Modoc's Tavern, Lake Outlet fish fry stand, and the impressively built Syracuse Yacht Club House—can be viewed in the Liverpool Library's local history photo collection

PLANTING HOPE AMID GRIEF

Who created that beautiful garden by Onondaga Lake Park?

You see them in the spring and summer, glorious as butterflies: teens in gowns and tuxes posing for prom pictures in May, followed by brides and grooms for wedding photos from June through September. It's a popular spot for photos, that flowering garden next to Onondaga Lake Parkway at the entrance to the village of Liverpool. But few read the signs or know the story behind the Butterfly Garden of HOPE or its sponsoring organization HOPE for Bereaved.

Early in the morning of August 21, 1977, Therese Schoeneck got a call: her 21-year-old daughter Mary had been in a car accident. When Schoeneck arrived at the hospital, she learned Mary was a passenger in a pickup truck that had split a telephone pole in half. The intoxicated driver's injuries were minor, but Mary was dead. "I wasn't prepared for grief," Schoeneck told the Syracuse *Post-Standard*. "I didn't understand." After the funeral, she was "screaming inside." Pastoral counselors and friends with similar experiences helped, but Schoeneck felt driven to establish a group for grieving parents to readjust to life.

She founded HOPE for Bereaved, a nonprofit that provides counseling, support, and social activities for those who've lost loved ones. In May 1992, their 14th year, they established the Butterfly

BUTTERFLY GARDEN OF HOPE

WHAT: A community garden and memorial

WHERE: 6751 Onondaga Lake Parkway, Liverpool

COST: Free to visit; can be rented for weddings and other events on an hourly basis

PRO TIP: To honor a loved one, you can dedicate a brick in the Garden; various sizes, including a photo memorial, are available at HopeForBereaved.com

Even in autumn, the garden is a place of peaceful reflection.

Garden of HOPE. Shaped like a butterfly with wings outstretched, the garden was planted with trees, 150 flowering shrubs, and hundreds of flowers. “The Butterfly is the universal symbol of hope,” said Schoeneck, “and everything we’re about is hope.” Plants and trees were donated by local nurseries and garden clubs. Contributions maintain and illuminate the garden. Today, benches, a gazebo, and a brick path give visitors a quiet, lush landscape in which to sit and reflect with a view of Onondaga Lake beyond.

HOPE for Bereaved provides services to thousands throughout Central New York with a help line (315) 475-HOPE and community education programs free of charge.

WHEN THE WALL CAME TUMBLING DOWN

Why is there a slab of broken concrete behind the MOST?

Talk about unbelievable job perks. Facebook and Google were once famous for them, but they never gave away pieces of history. One international company with an office in Syracuse did, and 33 years later, it's the perk that keeps on giving.

BettyAnn Kram worked for German-based Inficon Leybold Heraeus in 1989 during the fall of the Berlin Wall. "A colleague in Germany asked if I would be interested in some segments of the wall," Kram told the Syracuse *Post-Standard*. "They were built in three meter segments. That's an actual segment—that's how it was constructed." She said yes, not for herself but for the MOST, the new Museum of Science and Technology that she was helping to establish in Armory Square.

Three segments arrived in 1990. According to *Post-Standard* reporter Chris Baker, "Two of them were broken into pieces that were given to founding members of the MOST and even sold at the gift shop for a time." The third segment, 12 feet tall and 3 feet wide, became the focal point of a Peace Garden behind

MOST PEACE GARDEN

WHAT: A segment of the Berlin Wall

WHERE: Outside the southern wall of the MOST

COST: Free

PRO TIP: There is also a display inside the MOST that includes smaller pieces of the Berlin Wall.

For Syracuse Public Art Commission Chair Michael John Heagerty, it's a hidden treasure: "We need to show it off like we need to show off other history in Onondaga County."

the MOST. "The visible side was originally very colorful. That was the west side," Kram said. "The other side had nothing."

Though it came down in Berlin, in Syracuse, the wall segment stands as a dramatic visual illustration of divided East and West Germany and the Cold War.

Lifelong Syracuse resident Sharon Akkoul remembers the Berlin Wall from college: "My study abroad was Berlin in the fall of 1984, while the Wall still existed and there were two Germanies. I have found great peace and encouragement knowing a section of the Wall I may have walked by every day is here with me now."

The concrete monument at the MOST is one of just four segments in New York State. Others can be found around the world.

A segment of wall that once faced the West.

DEATH'S A BEACH

What paranormal reality show investigated an Oneida Lake resort?

After Sylvan Beach Amusement Park and a local restaurant changed ownership in 2007, it was rumored that, over time, employees, customers, and area residents had been experiencing more frequent ghost sightings and paranormal activity. Conveniently, this coincided with the heyday of paranormal investigation reality TV programming.

In 2012, at the end of the resort's summer season, one of the biggest franchises, SciFi's *Ghost Hunters*, came to Oneida Lake to videotape an episode. TAPS—The Atlantic Paranormal Society—visited both the amusement park and Yesterday's Royal, a restaurant housed in a restored hotel. One of the oldest structures at the beach, Yesterday's Royal and the amusement park were the focus of TAPS's daytime visits and overnight stays during a weeklong investigation from September 10 to 18. Employees past and present were interviewed, and three ghosts figured prominently.

Restaurant manager Pat Goodenow described how he'd heard "pounding on the walls . . . and there [was] no one in the building. We had bar glasses fly off the bar with no one apparently near them." He witnessed this late at night alone in the building, but customers also reported seeing a Victorian lady standing in a window looking out at the lake.

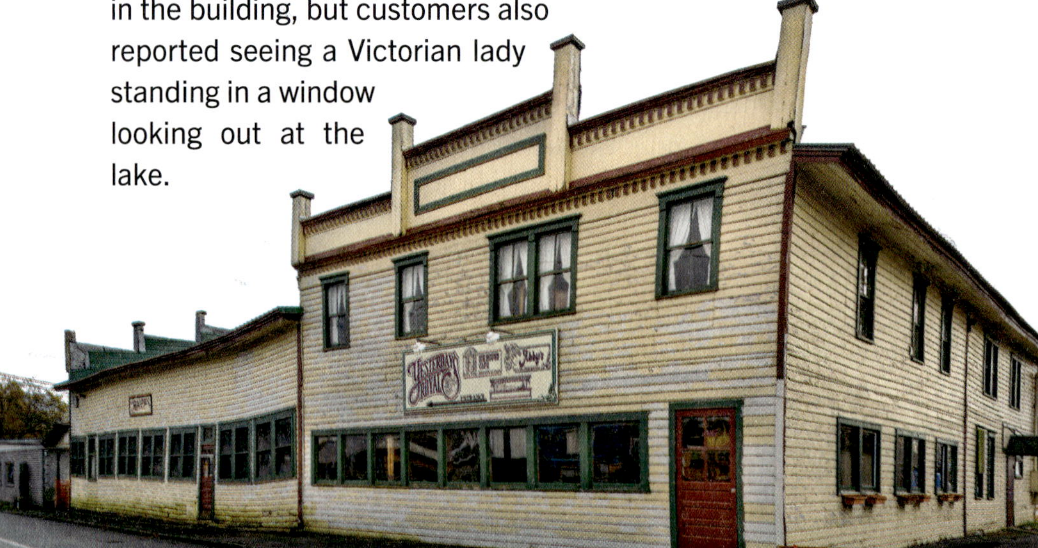

Yesterday's Royal and the roller coaster in the off-season.

Abby, the Victorian woman also known as the Lady in White, lingered in the hotel. Scotty, whose body was discovered in the Treasureland building, haunted the park and the Playland attic. A worker named Jack opened doors and made mischief at the bar. During the episode, knocking, whistling, metallic sounds, a loud bang, and something toppling over was heard at various locations. In the restaurant-hotel, there was an indication of a presence.

The conclusion was that the spirits were not malicious, but just having fun. The episode debuted February 27, 2013.

GHOST HUNTERS AT SYLVAN BEACH

WHAT: TAPS investigates an Oneida Lake resort

WHERE: Sylvan Beach Amusement Park and Yesterday's Royal Restaurant (now closed)

COST: Free park admission; fee for rides and games

PRO TIP: Park After Dark ghost tours begin at 9:30 p.m. More information is on their website at sylvanbeachamusementpark.com.

Airing as the mid-season finale of Season #9, *Ghost Hunters* Episode #185 investigated three ghosts—Abby, Scotty, and Jack—who died at the Sylvan Beach resort.

GRAND CANYON OF SYRACUSE

What urban setting feels both remote and otherworldly?

The city's most unexpectedly beautiful park is also its most hidden, tucked away in a steep-sided glen running through the city's hilly southwest corner. The narrow valley opens to a series of enchanting landscapes: broad swaths of green lawn; rustic stonework, including retaining walls, bridges, and staircases built nearly a century ago; and sloping woodlands that edge the neighborhoods of Strathmore and Elmwood.

The park's main draw is its picturesque stream. Capped by Corcoran High School to the west, the stream disappears underground at the eastern end near an old (circa 1850) stone mill. Overhung with trees and lined with walking paths, this spring-fed waterway is ironically called Furnace Brook despite its icy-cold temperature. On a hot summer day, kids—and dogs—wade to cool down. Standing beside Furnace Brook, former Syracuse Common Councilor Bob Dougherty noted, "Right here . . . you have no idea that you're in the city of Syracuse. All you can hear is the water. This is why people have called this the Grand Canyon of Syracuse."

The 65-acre, nearly half-mile-long park has abundant natural resources, including 70 species of trees and shrubs, wildflowers, birds, and other wildlife. Maple trees have been tapped for maple syrup through a Syracuse Parks and Recreation program.

The park is well traveled with walkers, runners, cyclists, and families with children, but like any isolated urban space, it's best visited during the day.

The steady sound of running water is the backdrop to this unexpected oasis. Courtesy of Linda Lowen.

ELMWOOD PARK

WHAT: A 65-acre urban oasis

WHERE: Glenwood Avenue 1/10th of a mile from South Avenue

COST: Free

PRO TIP: Near the entrance, read about Elmwood's early history as a resort called Dreamland Park.

The clear-running stream is home to freshwater shrimp. Each year, 400 brook trout from Carpenter's Brook Fish Hatchery join the existing population of wild brook trout and brown trout, making it an urban favorite for anglers.

Former Syracuse *Post-Standard* columnist Sean Kirst has compared its magic to Middle Earth: "[E]very day, I revisit Tolkien's world when I walk my dogs . . . It is reminiscent, to me, of Tolkien's Ithilien, a fallen garden touched by shadow, which becomes part of its beauty."

ARTS TAKE FLIGHT

If my flight is delayed, what's there to do at the airport?

Three letters—SYR—stand for an airport that's a hub of arts and education. Inside Syracuse Hancock International Airport, you'll discover an aviation museum, children's library, art gallery, and a place to pet a friendly dog. Even if you're not a ticketed passenger, you're welcome to visit.

Hidden underneath the main staircase is the Regional Aviation History Museum. The Onondaga Historical Association's interactive exhibits tell the story of transportation in Syracuse. There's a touch of steampunk glamor in the display of flight suits and leather aviator helmets that include those iconic goggles. Model airplanes depict legendary aircraft, and a Franklin automobile enjoys permanent airport parking. Watch *The Crossroads of Transportation* for a crash course on Syracuse history in under five minutes.

Remember visiting a bookmobile? The SYR Reading Runway—a unique partnership with the Onondaga County Public Libraries—is an actual children's library in the airport. Cute and cozy, it invites you to sit and read. Want to borrow a book? Just take it—no library card required and no overdue fines.

Syracuse's most inclusive art gallery, the SYR Community Art Program has more than 220 pieces on display. The 12" x 12" paintings—from artists at school districts, libraries,

SYRACUSE HANCOCK INTERNATIONAL AIRPORT

WHAT: An aviation museum, children's library, and more

WHERE: 1000 Col. Eileen Collins Boulevard

COST: Free, but there's a charge for airport parking

PRO TIP: The coolest airport attraction is the nose of a plane that you can climb into, complete with cockpit controls. It's in the terminal's southern end near Baggage Claim.

The SYR Community Art Program gallery.

advocacy groups supporting individuals with disabilities, youth organizations, juvenile detention centers, and senior living facilities—are examples of art with heart.

If flying makes you anxious, put your stress on "paws" with a little doggo-and-me time. PAWS of CNY brings experienced therapy dogs into the airport through the SYR PET (Pets Easing Travelers) Program. You may see them at baggage claim, over by TSA, or even at the gate. A popular pooch is Jay Peacock's dog Harley, a 110-pound Chesapeake Bay Retriever who looks like a big teddy bear. All PET teams wear yellow and are easy to spot.

Every March, kids and adults can enter the Poetry in Flight competition celebrating National Poetry Month in April. The adult winner gets two round-trip Delta Airlines tickets. Details at syrairport.org.

DIY HOUSE OF SPIRITS

What house has spirit closets and a dark room?

If you've ever acted impulsively and surprised others, you may have said, "The spirit moved me." For Timothy Brown, spirit did much more. It dictated plans for a house in a rural village that's known worldwide as Spirit House.

Born in Vermont, Brown moved to Georgetown in 1847, a middle-aged man with no experience as an architect or builder. In fact, the Georgetown Historical Society noted, "The entire community knew that Brown was no carpenter, but in about 10 years' time . . . the house was completed." He felled local timber, doing the construction himself. A master carpenter helped raise the frame and later told skeptical locals Brown had built "the best frame he had ever seen."

Author Melanie Zimmer has done extensive research into Spirit House. She says the idea came to Brown one night in an image from his dead sister Mary. One extraordinary feature—three tiers of sculpted eves in an elaborate pattern—is unique to Spirit House: "Their decorative details have been compared to inverted clock keys and icicles." Yet for Brown, "These were special eves . . . designed to be 'spirit closets' . . . to house spirits." Doorways, frames, and columns were scalloped, rounded, and nicked to discourage evil spirits. One interior room without windows, "the dark room," facilitated communication with the spirits.

Madis Senner, writing in *Wisdom* magazine, believes that "[w]hat also contributes to the divine nature of Spirit House is the thoughts, intentions of others that came there before . . . the

---

According to Syracuse *Post-Standard* Home and Real Estate editor Pam Lundborg, "British Broadcasting came . . . in 2005 to try to connect with the spirit of the late Mae West."

The intricate carvings are rumored to house spirits. Courtesy of Juan Junco.

creation of a vortex that begins to draw an increased amount of energy, essences or consciousness to a particular spot. A vortex . . . would indicate that prayer, ceremony or meditation occurred there. Spirit House has many vortices."

It also has many names: Brown's Temple, Brown's Free Hall, Ghost House, Mystery House, and—because of the fancy three-tiered eaves—Wedding Cake House.

BROWN SPIRIT HOUSE

WHAT: An ornate house purportedly built under spirit guidance

WHERE: 916 NY-26, Georgetown

COST: Free to view from the outside

PRO TIP: It's on the National Register of Historic Places, but has not been well-maintained. The Preservation Association of Central New York has listed it as "a threatened property."

SYRACUSE'S PLACE AT THE TABLE

What company was known by its product rather than its name?

What locals called Syracuse China was for many years a product of the Onondaga Pottery Company, not the company name itself. Founded in 1871 as a manufacturer of quality earthenware, O.P. Co. was overseen by Richard Pass who relocated from Staffordshire, England, to become superintendent in 1875. His son James came too. James, who'd grown up learning about pottery, studied analytical chemistry at Syracuse University to understand and overcome problems in pottery manufacturing. After Richard's death, he became superintendent in 1884.

O.P. Co. produced simple white tableware at its Fayette Street plant, but, in 1884, Elmer Walter established the Boston China Decorating Works across the street. When Walter's business burned down in 1886, he and his employees were hired by O.P. Co. to establish an in-house pottery decorating department.

In 1888, James Pass developed America's first truly vitreous china, the highest grade of chinaware. Starting in 1895, all pieces were marked with the "Syracuse China" backstamp. Hotels, restaurants, and railroad companies quickly became eager customers. In 1896, O.P. Co. developed a chip-resistant Round Edge shape. That same year, they installed the ceramic industry's first in-house lithographic shop for printing decals to

SYRACUSE CHINA AND ONONDAGA POTTERY COMPANY

WHAT: America's first vitreous china

WHERE: Formerly at 2801 Court Street

COST: Free to drive by

PRO TIP: Smith Restaurant Supply in DeWitt operates a vintage consignment shop where you can still buy Syracuse China pieces.

Left: The original factory of the Onondaga Pottery Company.
Right: Employees work on egg cups.

decorate Syracuse China. After 1897, O.P. Co. discontinued other products to manufacture only vitreous Syracuse China.

Moving into the 20th century, production increased, and a new Court Street plant was added. In the late 1930s, an airbrush design process further enhanced Syracuse China's appeal. During World War II, with men called off to war, women swelled the ranks of the workforce, producing almost 60 million pieces for the military. The shift to predominantly female workers became permanent. In 1966, Onondaga Pottery Company officially became Syracuse China, the name it operated under until the Syracuse factory closed in 2009.

The Onondaga Historical Association acquired the Syracuse China archive and historic china collection in 2009, encompassing more than 30 exhibit cases featuring rare pieces from the 138-year-old company.

THE DYNAMIC CERAMIC DUO

How did Syracuse China make electricity safer?

You don't have to be a fire chief to know that wood burns, yet in the early years of electricity, wood was used as an insulator for wiring devices because that's all they had. In the event of a short circuit, wood frequently caught fire, and wet wood didn't insulate as well as dry.

Albert Seymour, the superintendent of a Syracuse lighting company in 1888, was concerned that frequent shocks and fires would slow the expansion of electricity into homes, shops, and factories. He'd seen the development of a new ceramic at Syracuse's Onondaga Pottery Company under its new superintendent James Pass, and wanted to learn more about its properties.

An article from the *Syracuse Herald-Journal* on October 21, 1941, details what happened next: "Convinced by tests that the new pottery developed by Pass would make good insulation, Pass & Seymour in 1890 formed a partnership for the manufacture of electrical porcelain. Like the new product of the Onondaga Pottery Company, the electrical product was called at first Syracuse China. In the early years, Pass & Seymour manufactured many types of electrical porcelain."

Operating out of a former horseshoe factory, P&S's electrical porcelain circuit breakers and insulators helped make electricity usage safer and more widespread. In 1898, they expanded to produce electrical spark plugs for the emerging automotive industry. In 1900, a huge factory was built in Solvay.

At its peak, Pass & Seymour employed almost 1,000 people at its Milton Avenue factory, yet a decade after its 1984 sale to Legrand US, the Solvay factory was closed.

The James Pass Arboretum is one of Syracuse's lesser-known urban parks.

PASS & SEYMOUR'S ELECTRIC HISTORY

WHAT: How Syracuse China helped make electricity usage widespread

WHERE: Legrand maintains an office at 50 Boyd Avenue

COST: Visit the beautiful James Pass Arboretum instead for free.

PRO TIP: Gifted to the city by his widow, Pass Arboretum—though never developed as a true arboretum—was named a protected historic landmark in 1994 because of Pass's historical significance.

According to the Onondaga Historical Association, "By 1925, Pass & Seymour was recognized as one of the major manufacturers in Onondaga County, employing nearly 500 people. . . . In 1929, Richard Pass, was elected president of the company his father had founded." He was critical to the development of the Syracuse Secret Weapon, a nonmetallic land mine used during World War II.

BOMB IN A CHINA SHOP

What was the Syracuse Secret Weapon of World War II?

Landmines are effective only if undetected. In World War II, electronic minesweepers helped the enemy locate American mines. To avoid detection, the Army wanted a nonmetallic landmine that met critical specifications: it would detonate in soil and underwater, withstand the pressure of feet but explode under the weight of a moving vehicle, and operate between -40 and 170 degrees Fahrenheit. It also needed a specially designed chemical fuse.

Two Syracuse companies in partnership with each other—Onondaga Pottery Company (O.P. Co.) and Pass & Seymour, manufacturer of electrical wiring devices—worked with the army's ordnance department. Company president Richard Pass selected specialists from O.P. Co. and P&S for the project. Research began in March 1942, and the ceramic mine was developed in seven months. Over 400 tests were done at Highland Forest Park in Fabius.

The fuses were made by P&S workers, and O.P. Co. employees produced and built the anti-tank landmine. Another explosive device, the pocket mine, was developed as well. Soldiers could carry them in their pockets and use them as a hand grenade, booby trap, and demolition device.

SYRACUSE CHINA'S EXPLOSIVE WWII PRODUCTS

WHAT: Ceramic landmines that could avoid detection

WHERE: Built in Syracuse, tested at Highland Forest, Fabius

COST: Free

PRO TIP: The Onondaga Historical Association has one of these mines on display in their downtown museum.

The daughter of Richard Pass, Ruth Hancock was a child at the time. She recalled the Highland Forest testing: "One cold fall afternoon I watched an exploding mine hurl a huge steel

Highland Forest's picturesque Skyline Lodge belies the park's history as a testing site.

plate into the sky and heard my father's urgent yell: 'Run north everyone, run north.' Everyone scattered every which way."

Interviewed by Syracuse newspaper columnist Dick Case in 2011 during a visit to Highland Forest, Ruth "remembers more open land back then, maybe a farm house or barn . . . And that 'huge explosion.'" Case noted that a 1945 *Syracuse Herald-Journal* article "finally revealed the 'secret' invention of the ceramic mines" and Syracuse's role as a center of mine technology research.

Onondaga Pottery Company paused its production of cups, saucers, and tableware made of Syracuse China to manufacture an estimated 4 million landmines in 15 months.

GOOD VIBES ONLY

Why aren't there any Hotel Syracuse ghost stories?

Those looking for ghosts at the Hotel Syracuse won't find much. While newspaper accounts verify an occasional death here and there, apparently no restless spirits have stuck around. In fact, there's scant evidence of anything odd in its 100-year-old history. The only claim comes from a paranormal group inactive since 2016. Member Lillee Allee wrote, "A psychic claimed there was a male ghost in Room 517. . . . Staff reported doors opening or closing by themselves, phones ringing from empty rooms, and the feeling of someone in an empty corridor with them."

A 1984 article in the *New York Times* describes one unfortunate incident in an adjacent building no longer owned by the hotel: "A 31-year-old Syracuse man who had been celebrating New Year's Eve at the Hilton Tower fell 100 feet to his death." An elevator holding 15-20 passengers had stalled between floors; two men pried open its doors, jumped to the floor below, and began helping others exit. Another man jumped down and, after landing, lost his balance and fell backward down the elevator shaft.

On a happier note, those looking for celebrities will find plenty of Hotel Syracuse stories. Among the famous folks who've visited are US presidents Dwight Eisenhower, John F. Kennedy, Richard Nixon, Jimmy Carter, and Bill Clinton; aviator Charles Lindbergh; comedian Bob Hope; crooner Nat King Cole; and rock

Painted and coffered ceilings and murals inside the hotel.

'n' roll icons Elvis Presley and the Rolling Stones.

When John Lennon came to Syracuse in October 1971 for Yoko Ono's art exhibit at the Everson Museum, rumors swirled of a possible Beatles reunion. While the Fab Four didn't reunite, Ringo Starr and Eric Clapton jammed with Lennon for his 31st birthday in a room at the Hotel Syracuse.

HOTEL SYRACUSE STORIES

WHAT: The hotel's history of good vibes

WHERE: 100 East Onondaga Street

COST: Free to visit the lobby, fee for tour below

PRO TIP: Sign up for a Historic Hotel Syracuse presentation and tour through the Onondaga Historical Association to learn more about the hotel's famous visitors, including John Lennon.

WHAT LIES BENEATH

Is it true Syracuse has underground pedestrian tunnels?

One of Syracuse's most fascinating feats of mining and engineering isn't open to the public. In many ways, it's a time capsule back to 1967, the year it was built. For those who could care less about history, it marks an attempt to address the basic desire of every Syracuse resident once winter rolls around: *How do I get there from here without going through the cold and snow?*

Syracuse, it turns out, has underground pedestrian tunnels. Former Syracuse *Post-Standard* columnist Sean Kirst wrote about them back in 2015 during the $70-million restoration of the Hotel Syracuse. A tunnel from the hotel basement "turns into a walkway in the parking garage of the AXA Towers and ends at a tunnel that connects the Oncenter, the Mulroy Civic Center and the Onondaga County War Memorial."

At the time of its construction, it was a job done by hand. In 1967, according to the *Post-Standard*, "sandhogs . . . at work under S. Warren St." excavated the pedestrian tunnel 20 feet below street level, "averaging 16 inches a day in their mole operations." Standing on scaffolding in the 9' x 7.5' tunnel, they had to hold "pneumatic drills at hip level to chop through heavy sections of compacted gravel and pressure-hardened clay." Carving out the 56-foot walkway took 50 days. The $65,000 tunnel was a joint effort of Mutual of New York (MONY), Hotel Syracuse, and the City of Syracuse.

DOWNTOWN UNDERGROUND PEDESTRIAN TUNNELS

WHAT: An off-limits network of passages

WHERE: Between the Hotel Syracuse and points east

COST: Not open to the public

PRO TIP: Follow @SyracuseHistory on Instagram, TikTok, and Facebook—David Haas has posted a slew of photos of the Underground Tunnels and other insider places.

Inside one of the city's deepest secrets.

Seeing the space 48 years later, Kirst noted, "The hotel tunnel and the garage walkway both have a very 1960s feel, and the walkway retains evocative spaces that were built for subway-style advertising." While he thought the walkway would be appreciated "by convention visitors who want to dodge lousy weather," the Hotel Syracuse did not include the tunnel in its 2015 renovation plans.

The tunnel project was tiny compared to the original vision: an enclosed mall linking Hotel Syracuse with the former MONY Center, now occupied by AXA Towers and The Tech Garden.

JUST MY TYPE

Why did seeing words on the page spell S-A-L-E-S for the Smith Brothers?

If you lived in Syracuse in 1903 (a century before Tinder), the four Smith Brothers were your type, bringing innovation and prosperity, first with the founding of L.C. Smith & Bros. Typewriter Company in January, and second, with a new factory—a vast eight-story behemoth—at Washington and Almond Streets. The factory opened in September, but back in March, Lyman Smith had been so eager to get started, he'd directed a crew to dig the foundations before the architectural drawings were completed.

The key to the Smith Brothers' rise was their willingness to invest in change. Originally gun manufacturers, they'd pivoted to typing machines 15 years earlier, establishing the Smith Premier Typewriter Company in 1887. Invented by Alexander T. Brown, the double keyboard typewriter typed both uppercase and lowercase letters, and they'd sold over 60,000 by 1894. Yet the Smith Premier was a "blind" writing machine—typists couldn't see what they were typing. A new style was emerging—the "visible" typewriter—and that's the one they manufactured when they formed L.C. Smith.

The gamble paid off. By 1904, Syracuse had become known as Typewriter City, and, by 1911, the Washington Street factory had doubled in size. Yet they faced competition from another manufacturer, the Corona Typewriter Company 33 miles away in Groton. In 1906, Corona had introduced a lightweight portable typewriter. Ultimately, the two merged in 1926, establishing the world's largest typewriter company. The shortened Smith

---

An early company slogan was a play on the popular adage, "The pen is mightier than the sword, but the Smith Premier Typewriter bends them both!"

Top courtesy of CNY Chapter National Railway Historical Society. Inset courtesy of Onondaga County Public Library, New York Heritage Digital Collections.

L.C. SMITH & BROTHERS TYPEWRITER COMPANY

WHAT: The writing machine before computers

WHERE: Formerly at 701 E. Washington Street

COST: Free

PRO TIP: The Onondaga Historical Association Gift Gallery sells jewelry made from old typewriter keys—Tom Hanks has one of their tie clips.

Corona name became official in 1946. In 1955, they introduced the electric office typewriter and a portable model came out a year later.

But in 1960, manufacturing left Syracuse, and Smith Corona had quit the typewriter business by 2005. Maybe the Smith brothers should have stuck to their guns.

GEARING UP FOR THE FUTURE

What's the history of creativity in Syracuse's Near Westside?

When mechanical engineer Charles Lipe rented a building on Geddes Street for his machine shop, he found he had more space than he needed. So the 29-year-old inventor opened it up to other inventors. Today, the Lipe Shop would qualify as a business incubator or makerspace for bringing together like-minded entrepreneurs. However, back in 1880, few realized it would become Syracuse's cradle of industries by nurturing several "disruptive" innovators.

One of those was Alexander T. Brown, inventor of the Smith Premier Typewriter (and later a founder of Syracuse's Franklin air-cooled automobile company). Brown and Lipe became friends and collaborators, and, in 1894, they invented the Hi-Lo Bi-Gear, a two-speed bicycle gear. A year later, they formed the Brown-Lipe Gear Company to manufacture the product.

After the death of Charles Lipe

BROWN-LIPE GEAR

WHAT: A gear factory's then-and-now history

WHERE: 200 South Geddes Street

COST: Free to visit, admission fee for events

PRO TIP: Today's Gear Factory is home to art exhibits, showcases, live music, and outdoor performances. Events are listed at their website: TheGearFactorySyr.com.

The Gear Factory today.

in 1895, Brown modified the concept so it could be used in an automobile. He and Willard Lipe, Charles's brother, shifted Brown-Lipe from bicycle gear manufacturing to automotive technology. Soon they began to produce three-speed transmissions. Early customers included Franklin, the Yellow Cab Company, and Ford.

By 1906, Brown-Lipe Gear moved into a new five-story factory at the corner of West Fayette and South Geddes designed by architect Albert Kahn. Known for his "daylight factory" buildings, Kahn intentionally addressed the oppressive feel of dark sweatshops. The perimeter walls of his factories could be filled with glass to allow natural light into interior workspaces.

When the building changed hands over the next century, it lost its floor-to-ceiling windows. In 2015, Rick Destito spearheaded a $1.4 million restoration. He turned the former manufacturing plant into The Gear Factory, a live-work space for artists, musicians, creatives, and entrepreneurs, and now, the windows are back.

In 1910, Brown and Lipe created Brown-Lipe-Chapin with Winfield Chapin to manufacture automobile differentials, transmission gears, and clutches. In 1923, BLC became a division of General Motors.

LIPE OF LUXURY

What kid-friendly mansion once boasted a sledding trail a mile long?

From 1932 to 1934, during the worst years of the Great Depression, the largest private house in Syracuse was constructed atop one of the city's highest hills. Overlooking 400 idyllic acres, the $100,000 home was built by Marjorie Lipe Stacy, daughter of Syracuse industrialist Willard Lipe of Brown-Lipe-Chapin. Inside were numerous bedrooms, bathrooms with dazzling stained glass windows, a living room/ballroom, a ping-pong room, a sports room shaped like a ship, and a dining room that could seat 30. Outside was a marble aquarium, tennis courts, and a small zoo. A staff of seven—including a cook, chauffeur, butler, and maids—lived in the servants' quarters.

Despite its grandeur, it was perfect for kids. In 1929, the three Stacy children welcomed their three cousins—Bill, Suzanne, and Tip—into their family after Marjorie's brother W. Charles Lipe and his wife died in a boating accident.

Bill's daughter Pamela recalled her father describing it as "a really cool house" because they could play hide and seek for hours. In a short remembrance about his childhood there, Bill wrote, "A bobsled could start at the top of the hill and travel across Genesee Street, halfway up East Avenue. I know; I did it." The route would have been a wild ride roughly a mile long. Rumor has it that instead of a long trudge back home, the kids were picked up by the family chauffeur and driven back up the hill.

Look for the home's natural cooling system. Built before air conditioning, marble and tile in the hallway and the water in the former aquarium helped to keep the house cool.

Elegant details can be found throughout the house.

Suzanne's daughter Allison remembered her mother's stories of how the children would talk to each other through the pipes in the bathrooms "and say spooky things."

In 1944, the mansion sold for $45,000 and became Christ the King Retreat House. Fifty years later, the Roman Catholic Diocese of Syracuse assumed ownership and now operates it as a conference center.

CHRIST THE KING RETREAT HOUSE

WHAT: Once Syracuse's largest private home

WHERE: 500 Brookford Road

COST: Rental prices vary.

PRO TIP: While you can't sled down its hills anymore, the house is available for group rentals and corporate hide-and-seek bonding experiences.

BANKING ON FRANKLIN

What happened to Syracuse's most famous motorcar company?

If not for the Great Depression, South Geddes Street might have been another Detroit. That's where the Franklin automobile took shape, invented and designed by engineer John Wilkinson. His office sat next to the Lipe Machine Shop where parts for the car were first made. Wilkinson and industrialist Willard Lipe were joined by noted Syracuse inventor Alexander T. Brown and H. H. Franklin, a former newspaper publisher who manufactured the car and gave it his name. Together, they launched one of America's first automotive companies from within the Lipe Shop.

Still recognized as one of the most innovative designs of its time, Franklin cars featured Wilkinson's air-cooled engine and were comparatively lightweight. Describing the manufacturer's first model produced in 1902, Syracuse newspaper reporter Tim Knauss wrote that the "wood-bodied car . . . weighed 900 pounds and traveled up to 12 miles per hour."

Though viewed as a luxury car, the Franklin was easy and enjoyable to drive. According to Knauss, "Within four years, Franklin was the third-biggest manufacturer of cars in America.

THE FRANKLIN AUTOMOBILE

WHAT: An air-cooled car from one of America's first car companies

WHERE: Formerly on South Geddes Street

COST: Free

PRO TIP: See the early 1902 Franklin at the Onondaga Historical Association museum downtown and a later model at the airport's Regional Aviation History museum.

Courtesy of Onondaga County Public Library, New York Heritage Digital Collections.

The company grew to occupy 18 buildings with 34 acres of floor space at its campus on South Geddes Street. . . . During its peak in the mid-1920s, Franklin turned out nearly 15,000 cars a year and employed 3,500 people, making it the leading company in Syracuse."

The H. H. Franklin Club, a nonprofit membership organization for fans of the vehicle, credits its popularity to the "many body styles, both factory- and custom-made. . . . The Franklin's design . . . revealed its superior nimble handling, durability, economy and speed over the rough roads of the day."

Yet Knauss notes the company went bankrupt in 1934. The Franklin, although "lovingly crafted, could not compete with the cheaper models coming out of Detroit."

A "significant artifact in American automobile history," the first Franklin ever sold and the third one built is at the Onondaga Historical Association, on long-term loan from the Smithsonian.

AN INVENTOR, A DOCTOR, A SOY CANDLEMAKER

What prominent Syracusan's home was literally his castle?

Although Syracuse engineer and captain of industry Alexander T. Brown wasn't an architect, his wide-ranging interests earned over more than patents. The house he built in 1895—a red-hued stone castle of Potsdam sandstone (now rare) contained a central vacuum cleaning system and a hydraulic elevator. Allegedly when the elevator operated, nearby homes lost water pressure.

After Brown's death, the house became a medical office, then the home of Hueber Hares Glavin, an architectural firm. Now it's owned by Al Burch, a governance advisor, and Patti McDermott, an artist. Al and Patti discuss "the family" like they're blood relatives, especially Patti, who shares an old photo of Brown's two dogs sitting on the front seat of his Franklin automobile, the carriage house in the background: "The sad thing is the horse is peeking his head out as if he's saying, 'This is the future, and I'm the past.'" She's

ALEXANDER T. BROWN HOUSE

WHAT: A captain of industry's extraordinary 125-year-old home

WHERE: 726 West Onondaga Street

COST: Free to admire from the street. As this is privately owned, please do not trespass.

PRO TIP: To follow along with renovations and get an insider's take, follow The Alexander Brown House on Facebook.

Listed on the National Register of Historic Places in 1988, the Alexander T. Brown House is an example of Richardsonian Romanesque architecture and features a Spanish tile roof.

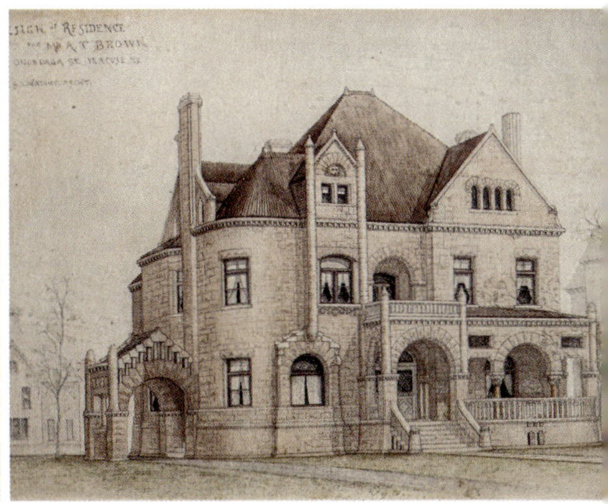

The castle in winter and an architectural rendering. Illustration courtesy of Patti Yates McDermott.

not wrong. The 5,500-foot building was later fitted with a car lift, housing 10 vehicles and a live bear.

Patti senses the spirit of Mary Margaret, the "the first lady" of the house, who "is wonderfully glad that we're here to keep the restoration going." Mary Margaret plays a little game: "I'd clean the kitchen counter off, walk out of the room, then come back to a penny sitting on the counter. It's like she's saying, 'Hey, I'm here.'" The house is also mischievous: "Things get moved. They disappear, then oddly reappear in the same place. . . . It makes me wonder: if you're married to a tinkerer, he himself must have been playful."

Outside, Patti has more playful companions, although these are living, breathing creatures. She feeds corn to crows who leave her dice, plastic bits, old bones, and other oddities she's collected in a bowl. They've inspired her business, Ravens Nest Candles.

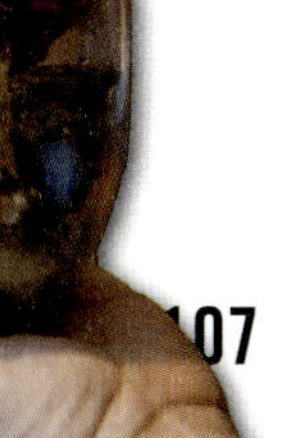

SYRACUSE'S LOST XANADU

What short-lived venue was promoted as America's finest nightclub?

Locals often complain that Syracuse has no good nightclubs. But for one shining moment during the Great Depression, the Cafe Dewitt—a dreamlike Art Deco pleasure palace—was advertised as "the world's most beautiful night club." Christened "The New Temple of Entertainment" by the *Syracuse Herald*, the Cafe Dewitt's crenelated walls rose in multiple tiers to a tower ablaze with light. Costing $250,000 (an estimated $27.8 million today), it opened on September 5, 1931.

JULIAN BROWN'S CAFE DEWITT

WHAT: The world's most beautiful nightclub built during the Depression

WHERE: Formerly at State Street and Erie Boulevard

COST: Free if you have a good imagination

PRO TIP: An internet search will kick up a Cafe Dewitt, but that's in the Dewitt Mall, a repurposed school building combining residential/retail space in Ithaca, NY.

Built atop a former lumberyard, this "remarkable achievement of modernistic architecture" was the vision of Julian Brown, playboy son of millionaire Syracuse inventor Alexander T. Brown. That summer, the *Herald* reported, "the unique building . . . sprang up with fantastic speed. . . . Persons who have been away from the city six weeks are rubbing their eyes when they pass by the corner and see . . . a design which is original in every respect."

Built by the Dawson Construction Company, the Cafe Dewitt was "executed entirely by Syracuse skill, Syracuse labor, and Syracuse materials." Both inside and outside, "panels of exquisite design are in black and silver. . . . Black velvet curtains of a rich quality cover the walls. . . . Outside the building will be under flood-illumination creating a kaleidoscopic effect as it

Cafe Dewitt. Courtesy of Onondaga Historical Association.

NEW YEAR'S EVE

Join the Gay Whirl of Merriment and Gaiety at

CAFE DEWITT

That will mark our New Year's party and usher in 1932 amidst the fun making of the smart coterie that will gather here. Our marvelous orchestra offers the latest dance hits. Favors for all the ladies.

Broadway Entertainers

$7.50 per person

Including Supper

YOU BETTER PHONE NOW FOR RESERVATIONS

2-6828
2-4322

CAFE DEWITT
ERIE BOULEVARD AT STATE ST.

blends with the silver and black panels of the walls."

Adding to its otherworldly appearance was the fact that it had no windows. The interior was lit "by an ingenious system of color combinations . . . with red, amber, green, blue, and white lights . . . producing an unusual blending of light and color."

It was Brown's attempt to make "a genuine contribution to the social life of this city." Yet two months later, Brown and his Dewitt Development Corporation went into receivership. The contents of the Cafe Dewitt were auctioned off in 1938, and by November 1939 the building was demolished.

Cafe Dewitt's sold-out September 5th, 1931, opening night had a floor show and an orchestra "[d]irect from Hollywood Gardens." The event was attended by 620 with more than 500 turned away.

INSIDE THE PRINTERS' STUDIO

What company in a historic arts building thrives under pressure?

Tell someone, "I have a studio at the Delavan," and the reaction borders on *Charlie and the Chocolate Factory* wonder: "What's it like inside?"

Technically, it's a historic multiuse, multistory, multibuilding complex on Syracuse's Near Westside. Owner Harold Kyle characterizes it as "a rambling building with labyrinthine hallways and wildly crooked floors." His other business—Boxcar Press, which he and Debbie Urbanski started in Minneapolis in 1998—was the Delavan's biggest tenant for years when he purchased the building in October 2020.

But the Delavan Studios is really a living museum of the creative process, an active workspace for everyone from solo entrepreneurs and side-gig professionals to businesses that fly under the radar but are quietly famous.

Boxcar Press is one example. The largest supplier of letterpress printing in the world, it produces high-end printing and supports the letterpress industry by providing materials to design centers and individuals passionate about the art form. Plus, it's a global wholesale seller of printing plates and paper to more than 10,000 letterpress printers. When Boxcar was featured in *Martha Stewart Weddings* magazine, the business exploded, leading Boxcar to establish Bella Figura specifically

---

Originally the Syracuse Chilled Plow factory, it became an arts center when former IBM systems analyst Bill Delavan started renting unused space to artists in the building his father owned.

Boxcar's letterpress equipment.

DELAVAN STUDIOS AND BOXCAR PRESS

WHAT: An arts/business complex anchored by the world's biggest letterpress printer

WHERE: 509 West Fayette Street

COST: $5 to visit during the annual Holiday Open Studios

PRO TIP: During the above event, Boxcar sells fine letterpress cards, notebooks, wrapping paper, and other high-end goods at deep discounts. Make a beeline there first.

for wedding invitations. As Kyle said in a 2019 interview, "After Martha Stewart . . . we felt like we could do the impossible."

His MBA from the Sloan School of Management at MIT busts any stereotype of the starving artist, yet Kyle still takes artistic risks. He's the caretaker of a one-of-a-kind machine that cuts and packages little pieces of splicing tape for 8-millimeter film. The previous owner sent out 24,000 of these presstape packets each year to film companies, collectors, and archivists trying to preserve aging film strips. Built by Kodak 70 years ago, the presstape machine now lives—and reluctantly works—at the Delavan.

DEATH OF A ONCE-HAPPY VALLEY

Why did a farming community disappear into the wilderness?

Legend and lore used to be spread by word of mouth. Now the internet does it faster, amplifying the sensational at the expense of the truth. In the case of Happy Valley, rumors can turn a quiet, rural wildlife preserve into a haunted town depopulated by disaster and death.

> **HAPPY VALLEY WILDLIFE MANAGEMENT AREA**
>
> **WHAT:** An abandoned hamlet now a wildlife preserve
>
> **WHERE:** Off US Route 104 and County Route 26 in Williamstown, NY
>
> **COST:** Free
>
> **PRO TIP:** Looking for the haunt rather than the hunt? Start at the Happy Valley/Fraicheur Cemetery on Happy Valley Road.

Established in 1850, Fraicheur (pronounced Fraser) was a tiny hamlet straddling two towns, Albion to the west and Williamstown to the east. Its main street was Happy Valley Road, the dividing line between the two. The community was known for hops farming. Ninety years later, it was abandoned.

In 1998, Albion town historian Florence Gardner wrote, "This little settlement disappeared completely. . . . One person told me an epidemic of 'black water fever' struck, and killed many people. The ones who survived got out."

Historian and folklorist Michael Kleen recounts the legends of Happy Valley: "Locals whisper that the town was abandoned after Malaria or Small Pox swept through the area, or that a witch cursed the town, or it is haunted by the ghost of a Civil War soldier with a hook hand."

The truth is much more prosaic. The stock market crash in 1929 and crop failures led to property foreclosures. According

The only things that go bump in the night are wildlife.

to NewYorkUpstate.com reporter Scott Schild, "Happy Valley was cleared from the map. . . . The Department of Environmental Conservation stepped into the area and determined its use would be better as a wildlife management area." The government purchased property, freeing residents to move out. Many had already left during the Great Depression.

Most of Happy Valley has vanished into the wooded undergrowth. All that remains are the ruins of the schoolhouse founded in 1867 and the cemetery founded in 1866.

At just under 8,900 acres, hiking, hunting, trapping, fishing, and wildlife viewing are the featured activities at this site managed by the NYS Department of Environmental Conservation.

SURVIVING THE "FIST OF GOD"

How bad was the Labor Day Storm?

Central New Yorkers know how to hunker down and weather the worst of storms in the winter. Yet the storm everyone talks about—the one that did far more damage than any snowstorm in memory—was the Labor Day Storm. Fortunately, most people were asleep just past 1 a.m. on Monday, September 7, 1998, although that meant few heard the severe thunderstorm warnings issued moments before.

When the storm hit Syracuse at 1:15 a.m., winds ranged between 70-90 miles per hour, with gusts reaching 115 miles per hour. Lightning strikes of 10-20 per minute created an unearthly strobe-light effect across the landscape. Rain pummeled the area, accumulating an inch in less than an hour. The *Syracuse Herald-American* reported that for one Syracuse University student looking out a window, "[I]t seemed like the fist of God was here." A quarter-million customers lost power, many for over a week. Tens of thousands of trees fell, hitting buildings and blocking streets, and downed live wires added to the danger. Two large antennas just south of I-481 in DeWitt collapsed, interrupting local radio broadcasts. Three people died from injuries sustained during the storm.

Violent winds slammed into St. Lucy's Church, toppling its 100-foot steeple. It also destroyed the fourth story of the Delavan Center, leveling portions down to the third floor where acclaimed painter Jerome Witkin's studio was a total loss. Newspaper

---

According to the National Weather Service, this "long lived severe convective wind system or derecho" produced "a damage swath 10 to 12 miles long and nearly 30 miles wide."

Power utility trucks were a common sight. Courtesy of Mary Gualtieri.

columnist Dick Case spotted him in the parking lot, working on a painting commissioned for a Hollywood film. Artist Arlene Abend lost sculptures and equipment. She told Case she was devastated: "Right now it looks so insurmountable. I don't know if I can start again."

Officials who toured the area and reviewed damage surveys declared Onondaga County a federal disaster area. Ultimately damage totals came to $100 million.

THE LABOR DAY STORM

WHAT: A September 7, 1998, derecho packed winds up to 115 mph

WHERE: Across Syracuse and Onondaga County

COST: $100 million

PRO TIP: The National Weather Service's 1998 Labor Day Derecho page has extensive details and photos.

A-TISKET, A-TASKET

What winter work occupied Liverpool a century ago?

Today's gig economy work brings to mind shopping for Instacart, driving for Uber, and delivering food for GrubHub. But Liverpool's history of seasonal work and the side hustle came first. Its industries, though legendary, are now forgotten by many. Unique handcrafted products made Liverpool famous in the 1800s thanks to its industrious citizens and their gig-economy work ethic.

This particular side hustle started with John Fischer, a German immigrant who'd come to Syracuse to work in the salt industry. He saw that nearby swamps were thick with willow bushes that resembled a type of willow used in Germany to weave baskets. He began to focus on basket-making in 1852, envisioning large numbers of weavers inexpensively producing strong, sturdy baskets, and wrote back to those he knew in Germany. A good living could be made in America between the summer salt industry and winter basketmaking. Many joined him, making laundry baskets for his cottage industry, and the weavers were prolific, shipping out more than 360,000 baskets in just 1892 alone.

Basketmaking was a multistep process: First, willow branches were harvested and brought to a commercial steamer; the heat processing killed insects and made leaf removal and bark peeling easier. Liverpool families had two-story sheds built behind their homes. Upstairs the processed branches were stored.

LIVERPOOL WILLOW BASKETS

WHAT: Handcrafted baskets that are the legacy of Liverpool

WHERE: Liverpool Museum inside the Gleason Mansion, 314 Second Street, Liverpool

COST: Free but donations appreciated

PRO TIP: Look around Liverpool for those two-story "garages"; they're really old willow sheds, providing a glimpse into the provenance of the homes/properties they occupy.

Inside the Liverpool Museum at the Gleason Mansion.

Downstairs, in a space heated by a stove, the whole family gathered to peel branches and weave baskets. The industry thrived until the 1920s when the promise of a steady paycheck lured people away to factory work. Commercial basket weaving ended in the 1960s.

The Liverpool Museum at the Gleason Mansion showcases the handcrafted artistry of Liverpool residents of old. Next door is the seasonal Willow Museum housed in an old weaving shed. Both are operated by the Historical Association of Greater Liverpool.

Outside the Gleason Mansion is a century-old streetlamp from that other Liverpool—Liverpool, England, birthplace of the Beatles—a gift to Central New York's Liverpool.

FIVE FEET FROM DEATH

Did a plane crash into Onondaga Lake?

It's common knowledge that shipwrecks litter the bottom of Onondaga Lake. But there's also an Air National Guard F-94 jet 60 feet deep in the muck. It crashed due to a commonplace weather event in Syracuse. In a car, it's dangerous. In a plane, it's lethal.

At 9 a.m. on November 26, 1955, Lt. John Kesel took off from Hancock Field on an air defense mission, piloting a 138th Fighter Squadron jet. A second jet accompanied him, piloted by Captain John Etherington with Captain Larry E. Sander as radar observer. After the mission was completed, the three men headed back, Kesel leading the two-plane formation.

Sander told the Syracuse *Post-Standard* a snow squall had created zero visibility and Etherington was flying on instruments: "We had lost 1300 feet. As Lt. Kesel's plane was just about to hit I noticed the water." Sander yelled to Etherington to pull up the plane, and "we missed the water by about five feet." Kesel crashed his plane at 9:45 a.m., dying instantly.

ONONDAGA LAKE'S JET CRASH

WHAT: The wreckage of an Air National Guard F-94 jet

WHERE: Somewhere underwater off Lake View Point

COST: Free

PRO TIP: Once considered one of the most polluted lakes in the nation, the cleanup of Onondaga Lake was completed in 2016, but it's still not advised to scuba or swim.

A Le Moyne College junior, Kesel graduated flight school at Webb Air Force Base, Texas, in 1953 and logged 700 flight hours. His body was recovered the day after the crash.

Few know that the wreckage of a fighter jet lies beneath these serene waters.

Experts believe the squall disoriented Kesel and blamed the crash on vertigo caused by lack of a visible horizon. While vertigo only lasts for a few seconds, "in a jet going 375 miles an hour, if near the ground, the few seconds are not available for recovery. At 15,000 feet . . . there would be time to recover."

Sander told the newspaper, "when flying in formation at near wing tips, the pilot of the second plane is watching the first . . . to lead the way, and it's apt not to be on the lookout for obstacles or . . . a drop in elevation." Sander's quick reaction saved the two men.

OH MY DARLING HILL OBSERVATORY

Where's a good place to go stargazing?

Bring a winter coat, even in summer. At least dress warmly in long pants and boots in case of dew. If you're carrying a flashlight, cover the lens with a red balloon. If these behaviors sound odd, you've never been high atop the chilly hillside south of the city where the Syracuse Astronomical Society has its star parties. And if you haven't gone to one of their Free Public Observing Nights, you're missing out on one of the great wonders of the universe right in your own backyard.

You'll have to drive half an hour outside Syracuse, but the trip is worth it. The SAS holds monthly viewing events on clear summer nights down in Vesper, a hamlet south of the city in the hills of Tully. The dark skies in Vesper offer incredible views without urban/suburban light pollution, and the star parties are scheduled around the time of the new moon to optimize stargazing.

At the Vesper site is Darling Hill Observatory, built in 1971 and housing a 16" Newtonian reflecting telescope under a retractable roof that rolls back so the telescope is open to the night sky. View surface features of the moon and nearby planets, see the rings of Saturn, star clusters, nebulae, galaxies, and more. An observing deck allows a group to gather around the telescope and take

SYRACUSE ASTRONOMICAL SOCIETY'S VESPER SITE

WHAT: Public viewing nights at Darling Hill Observatory

WHERE: 485 Strong Road, Tully

COST: Free viewing nights are held April to November.

PRO TIP: Be sure to read the current year's online brochure at syracuse-astro.org. The Public Observing Tips will help you plan for a successful visit to see the stars.

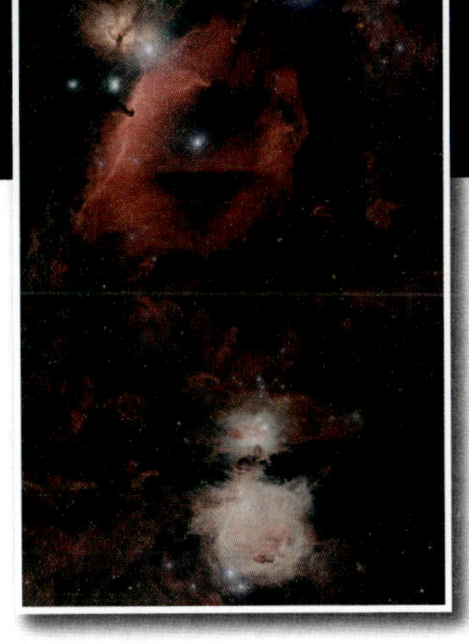

Heavens above! Top courtesy of Anthony Krishock. Inset courtesy of Kevin Weigel.

turns viewing, while a rolling ladder enables each individual to get up to the level of the eyepiece to see. Volunteer staff members guide visitors in locating objects in the sky.

Darling Hill's seven acres of land are remote, making it easier to become dark-adapted to the night sky. That's why red-balloon-covered flashlights are necessary, or bring a red flashlight to preserve night vision.

If you already own a telescope or binoculars, Darling Hill Observatory has concrete pads and accessible outlets, so you can take advantage of a stable viewing base with electricity.

KEEP ON TRUCKIN'... JUST NOT HERE

Why is the bridge on Onondaga Lake Parkway so low?

It's no secret—just Syracuse's trickiest problem: tractor-trailers hitting the low-clearance iron railroad bridge on Onondaga Lake Parkway.

It happens several times a year, enough that a recent Syracuse *Post-Standard* headline reflected the community's casual exasperation: "Yes, another truck just hit the Onondaga Lake Parkway railroad bridge." The *Post-Standard* website syracuse.com followed it up with a YouTube video, *A Brief History of Syracuse's Notorious Onondaga Lake Parkway Bridge*, laying out the facts. Along Onondaga Lake Parkway, several prominent signs announce LOW BRIDGE: 10 feet, 9 inches. They're often ignored. The average height of a tractor-trailer is between 13 and 14 feet. Typically, the cab gets through, but the trailer is either crumpled, wedged in, or knocked sideways. It's so commonplace, it's become a meme. Some have called the bridge "the undefeated heavyweight champion of Central New York."

The problem has been going on for decades. On November 11, 1952, an empty refrigeration truck driven by John Chapin of Kingsville, Ontario, hit the bridge. In 1958, it was hit twice in the same month, first by a driver from Providence, Rhode Island, second by a driver transporting furniture from Jacksonville, Florida. But officials took notice in 2010 when a double-decker

---

After the railroads came through, a bridge was built of "wrought iron plates and angle irons riveted together" in 1871. The *Syracuse Daily Journal* called it "beautiful, substantial, and permanent."

Know your height! Stay well below 10 feet, 9 inches.

ONONDAGA LAKE PARKWAY BRIDGE

WHAT: A frequent accident site that snags tractor trailers

WHERE: Along the Onondaga Lake Parkway

COST: Free

PRO TIP: When an accident happens, the lane is closed down for a couple of hours. It's best not to rely on this particular roadway if you have a time-sensitive appointment.

Megabus driver, using a personal GPS, which the company disavows, crashed into the bridge, killing four passengers. That triggered a new round of debates.

The 150-year-old bridge is low by today's standards because it was built to cross the Oswego canal, which connected Liverpool's salt industry and willow basket production to the Erie Canal. After the Oswego canal was abandoned in 1918, civic leaders pushed for a new roadway to encourage lakefront tourism as pollution of Onondaga Lake had impacted its once-popular shoreside resorts. A new parkway "for pleasure vehicle traffic only" was opened in 1932.

TWO TOWERS, TWO WOMEN

Why is a rusted steel column outside the DeWitt Town Hall?

It's battered and twisted, 21 feet high, and weighs six tons. It could be just another piece of construction debris except for its history. It's from the September 11, 2001, collapse of the World Trade Center. Today it's a memorial in front of the DeWitt Town Hall because of two women's dedicated endeavors: Pat Masten's community service and Arlene Abend's artistic vision.

Masten was known locally as the Flag Lady for her civic pride efforts, including getting a flagpole erected in DeWitt. When the Twin Towers fell, she told Syracuse *Post-Standard* reporter Michelle Breidenbach "it was an attack on all of us, every little town and village." Masten wanted to obtain "something that shows the destruction, either burnt or bent," to serve as a reminder. Through a series of phone calls and letters, she enlisted local politicians, eventually convincing then-NYC mayor Rudy Giuliani who promised a piece of debris. Months later, Breidenbach wrote, "She was told she could have a piece of steel. It was going to weigh 6 tons. And she had to pick it up in one week. At her expense." Masten wrangled a flatbed truck for transport, temporary storage in the DeWitt highway garage, and more than a thousand contributions of time, supplies, and money totaling $60,000.

TOWN OF DEWITT 9/11 MEMORIAL

WHAT: A steel column from the World Trade Center

WHERE: Outside the DeWitt Town Hall, 5400 Butternut Drive, East Syracuse

COST: Free

PRO TIP: Read the text on the memorial to learn how fire service members who lost their lives that day are honored. Incorporating pieces of rubble, it's overlooked but deserves attention.

Remembering those who were lost.

Sculptor Arlene Abend was commissioned to create the memorial. Back in 2001, Abend was 70 and Masten was 68. Though Masten passed away in 2019, Abend was 90 on the 20th anniversary of 9/11. "I wanted something simple and strong," she told Newschannel 9 WSYR reporter Andrew Donovan, reflecting on her role. "When I did it, it was a job. . . . It was problem-solving. And now, it's a very special place. . . . Being a part of it now seems more important than it was then."

Mounted halfway up the twisted column, Arlene Abend's stainless steel sculpture continues to challenge viewers. Does it represent a pair of hands? A flame? The two towers?

AREA 315 AND EXPLOSIVE D

Was there really a secret bomb plant during World War II?

Three months after Germany declared war on the US, in early 1942, the federal government took more than roughly 6,800 acres in the town of Lysander. The 250 families living there were evacuated, and roads through the area were blocked off. A month later, construction workers swarmed the site. Up to 3,000 people worked on a highly secretive facility containing 88 buildings and more than 20 miles of roads. Completed in May 1943, it was surrounded by 10 miles of chain-link fence, complete with guard towers and floodlights.

Just as mysterious as Nevada's Area 51 but less well known, this was the New York Ordnance Works. A US government-owned war project, it was designed to produce 60,000 pounds of ammonium picrate per day, seven days a week. Ammonium picrate—also known as dunnite or Explosive D—was used in armor-piercing artillery shells. To manufacture Explosive D, 8,000 employees—men and women—worked three shifts round the clock. Security at the plant was high. Everyone was searched before entering.

Those working with ammonium picrate had to take extra precautions. Inside one of three changing facilities, they removed all their civilian clothes, including underwear, then put on a work uniform: long johns, white "powder suit," gloves, cap, and shoes with soles that conducted away static charge, all to

---

Workers who were accidentally splashed with acid would run to a safety shower and pull the cord; allegedly, under the flow of water, the already-disintegrating clothes washed right off.

Concrete structures are the only reminders of the mysterious ordnance plant.

NEW YORK ORDNANCE WORKS

WHAT: A secretive government plant that produced Explosive D

WHERE: Roughly 13 miles north of Syracuse and 1 mile northeast of Baldwinsville

COST: Free

PRO TIP: A historical marker commemorates the former site where only remnants of the buildings remain. Look for it at 8233 NY-631 in Baldwinsville.

prevent accidental explosions. After their shift, everything was left in a laundry box. A shower was mandatory before putting on street clothes.

Buildings that produced Explosive D had escape chutes for evacuation in case of emergency. What looked like funhouse slides were a matter of life or death.

Yet by March 1944, manufacturing ended, and the facility was shut down. The federal government began to sell off the land in 1946. Decades later, Radisson was built atop the former ammonium picrate area.

EERIE ON ERIE

Who haunts the Erie Canal Museum?

Deceased sailors are often dispatched to a watery grave, but for the ghosts of the Erie Canal Museum, four feet of water—the original depth of the canal in 1825— wasn't enough to keep them down. The apparitions associated with the museum's Weighlock Building are restless and have made museum staff and visitors restless too.

Dan Ward, a former curator, remembers an incident in his office during his first week at the museum in 2009, when "a man walked up and stood in my doorway . . . I asked him if I could help. . . . He was translucent. He turned around and walked away . . . maintain[ing] his translucent form."

One of the other active spirits is described by Ward as a woman who is believed to have drowned. According to legend, her family's boat was in the weigh chamber

GHOSTS OF THE ERIE CANAL MUSEUM

WHAT: The Museum's Weighlock Building spirits

WHERE: 318 Erie Boulevard East

COST: $10 admission

PRO TIP: If you prefer sweet over scary, the Museum's Gingerbread Gallery is a longstanding holiday tradition with gingerbread entries submitted by kids, families, seniors, and professional bakers.

when she apparently fell into the water. The suction of the draining water—the means by which they weighed the boat—was strong enough to pull her under.

Another set of ghostly visitors was sighted by museum associate JP Body who first learned of the spectral children from a local attorney who was a regular visitor. As Body told *Eagle News* reporter Russ Tarby in 2011, the man asked, "'Have you seen the kids?' I said, 'Sure . . . I see lots of kids here.' He said, 'No. I mean the kids.' And I still didn't know what he meant. 'Don't worry,' he said. 'You will.'" Two weeks later, on a quiet Sunday morning, Body heard children laughing and talking loudly. Anticipating visitors, he looked up and saw two or three children outside; their clothing—calico, checkered shirt, straw hat, a bonnet—stood out. Though it was a fleeting glimpse, he realized they also were transparent.

In the Locktender's Garden, people have reported seeing two men arguing; if interrupted, they'll pick fruit from a nearby apple tree and throw it. Once launched, both apples and men disappear.

CUTS LIKE A KNIFE

What village pitched in during World War II to arm everyone from engineers to Marines?

If you lived through 9/11, you know how the world changed afterwards. In Camillus, one longtime manufacturer was hit hard. When knives were banned on flights after the terrorist attacks, and millions stopped carrying pocketknives, Camillus Cutlery Company experienced death by a thousand cuts.

Started by Charles Sherwood in 1896, Camillus made small pen knives with a staff of 20 cutlers until 1902, when New York City businessman Adolf Kastor bought the company. A German immigrant who imported German-made knives, Kastor had been hurt by an 1897 tariff raising rates as high as 57 percent. His solution: make knives in Camillus. By 1910, he grew the company to 200 employees. Good wages attracted expert workers from Germany, but in a village of less than a thousand, housing became a problem. His solution: build a dormitory for its bachelor employees.

CAMILLUS CUTLERY COMPANY

WHAT: One of America's biggest knife manufacturers

WHERE: Formerly at 54 West Genesee Street, now retail and residential space Camillus Mills

COST: Free

PRO TIP: Grab a cup of coffee at Camillus Mills' Freedom of Espresso and use their Wi-Fi to browse the Collectors of Camillus excellent website on Camillus knives.

After the war, character knives became popular. Designs featuring the Lone Ranger, Daniel Boone, Davey Crockett, and Dick Tracy appealed to kids.

Today the old factory is home to both retail and residential space.

Anticipating orders as World War II loomed, the company landed a contract for Navy jackknives in 1940. The Army, Marines, and Air Corps followed, but fulfilling so many orders seemed impossible. His solution: get the community involved. In the book *Camillus: The American Story of a Small Business,* historian Alfred Lief wrote, “The factory . . . was its natural channel for patriotic expression. Whole families . . . swung into action.” Teachers worked school vacations. Housewives took part-time shifts. A local clergyman assisted with shipping. The dedication paid off. By August 1943, just under 6.5 million knives had been produced.

Camillus thrived during peacetime as the world’s leading private label manufacturer of quality sporting and pocketknives. Folding knives were commonplace as knives up to four inches in length were allowed on aircraft. Then 9/11 happened, and the ban on knives cut the company deep. Cheaper imported Chinese knives also impacted business. In February 2007, Camillus Cutlery closed its doors for good.

WE ARE FAMILY

What's up with those striking—and similar—Victorian houses?

Syracuse has something in common with San Francisco — a lovely family of homes, smaller in number but bigger in square footage. In San Francisco, the colorful Victorian houses located at 710-720 Steiner Street across from Alamo Square go by various names: the Painted Ladies, Postcard Row, or the Seven Sisters. Here in Syracuse, our landmark row of homes is simply known as the Five Sisters.

Along the 300 block of Park Avenue just west of downtown Syracuse, the Five Sisters face Leavenworth Park. Built by George Brown as two-family homes in 1893-94, all are similar in style on the outside, each one crowned by a turret.

Back in 2009 when the houses were newly renovated and for sale, Syracuse *Post-Standard* reporter Greg Munno wrote, "[T]hese are big homes with porches and a park view on a tranquil street that has the feel of an older, mature suburb." Home and Real Estate editor Pam Lundborg recalled how this "row of ornate Victorian homes—each with a signature turret at the top—had fallen into seemingly hopeless disrepair . . . vacant,

peeling and crumbling," until utility company Niagara Mohawk stepped up in 2001, announcing a million-dollar restoration involving other community partners. Eventually, all dropped out due to lack of money, and the project stalled until the nonprofit housing agency Home Headquarters bought the homes in 2007. They renovated the exteriors and sold them to Syracuse construction company Time Cap in 2008, which did a gut rehab, tearing out the interiors and coming up with a different design inside each structure.

When Time Cap originally sold the homes between 2009 and 2010, they ranged in price from $185,000 to $240,000. One came back on the market in 2016, listing for $190,000 and selling for $171,000.

Time Cap bought the houses because "we were looking for a signature project," explained company president Jim Raite. They certainly found it. The Five Sisters are featured on their website.

FIVE SISTERS

WHAT: A row of Victorian houses

WHERE: 300 block of Park Avenue

COST: Free to view from the sidewalk

PRO TIP: While no public tours are offered, keep checking Zillow; you might get lucky and buy one for yourself.

These sisters don't need no misters.

PUT YOUR FOOT IN IT

Where and by whom was that thing that measures your shoe size invented?

In 1925, a Syracuse University student invented a simple but life-changing device that few recognize by name, but if you wear shoes, you've put your foot in it. It's still manufactured here nearly a century later. To build his first working model, he used a childhood Erector set. And because of his device, most people wear shoes that fit. Charles Brannock made measuring the length, width, and location of the arch of the foot easy and quick. His Brannock Device revolutionized the fitting of shoes.

THE BRANNOCK DEVICE

WHAT: The aluminum foot-measurement tool

WHERE: Invented in Syracuse and manufactured at 116 Luther Avenue, Liverpool

COST: Free to use at any shoe store

PRO TIP: Knowing the length of your foot, the width, and the length from the heel to the ball of the foot to determine the location of the arch will ensure you get the best fit possible.

Charles was the son of Otis Brannock who, along with Ernest N. Park, founded the Park-Brannock shoe store in Syracuse. Alongside shoes for men, women, and children, the store sold accessories such as hats and handbags, becoming so successful that it moved into a six-story building and was one of the East Coast's finest shoe stores.

Charles grew up working summers and weekends in the store. At SU, he sought to improve foot measurement, believing that "[t]he shoe salesman, like a doctor, has a distinct responsibility to his customers. A mistake in the fitting of a shoe . . . can easily endanger a person's health. The crippled feet of today are the misfitted feet of yesterday."

It took him two years to move from the Erector set model through ones made of cardboard, wood, then cast aluminum. Manufacturing began in 1925, and the Brannock Device

Brannock Devices old and new at the factory where they're still made.

was awarded a patent in 1928. Charles never married, never left Syracuse, and came to work every day through the 1980s. He died in 1992 at the age of 89.

Today, a million Brannock Devices—made of steel and relatively unchanged from the original—have been sold and are used in shoe stores worldwide.

The Smithsonian's Invention Stories website notes that the Brannock Device's "impact on the health and comfort of men and women serving in World War II was particularly notable."

FURS, EXPLOSIVES, CADILLACS, AND BEER

What's the history of Radisson and its "pioneers"?

Radisson—anointed "an Upstate 'New Town'" in 1977 by the *New York Times*—was intended as a "planned unit development community" when the NYS Urban Development Corporation bought the 2,000-acre parcel in 1969. The plan was to mix single-family homes with townhouses, patio homes, condominiums, and apartments, but for years the housing initiative stalled. The *Syracuse Herald-American* likened 1974-era Radisson to a "pioneer outpost with only a handful of families," but by December 1977 noted that it "will have more than 1,000 settlers toasting the beginning of 1978."

If those settlers did raise a glass on New Year's Eve, beer would have been the appropriate beverage, because that's what spurred growth. Following the Jos. Schlitz Brewing Company's 1976 purchase of more than 200 acres in the 900-acre Radisson industrial park for a regional brewery, interest in the community was reignited. In March 1977, the *Times*, citing its "superior land-planning and design standards," praised Radisson for "already producing visually distinctive contemporary and traditional housing." Like the *Herald-American*, the *Times* article labeled early residents "a 'pioneer' population of 150 families," adding that a future residential population in the thousands was anticipated. Today, with its manicured lawns and parklike setting, Radisson is the furthest thing from the wilderness.

The name Radisson comes from the 16th-century French explorer Pierre-Esprit Radisson, one of the founders of the Hudson's Bay Company famous for fur trading.

An architectural sculpture at the main entrance is a nod to the site's former life as an ordnance plant.

RADISSON COMMUNITY

WHAT: A planned residential/commercial "new town"

WHERE: Willett Parkway, Baldwinsville

COST: Free to walk through its public trails

PRO TIP: As an HOA community, Radisson's 7,000 residents abide by community guidelines and standards established to preserve the value of the homes.

Radisson's provenance is illustrious. John Jacob Astor—who'd made a fortune in the fur trade and in land speculation—acquired the acreage after the Revolutionary War. Astor sold it to the federal government, which built and briefly operated the New York Ordnance Works during World War II. Records indicate that in 1968, the Astor Estate again owned the land, which was acquired by Sol and Joseph Spector, father and son owners of Spector Cadillac, who sold it in 1969.

ART OF GLASS

What under-recognized artist ran a "leading" design studio in Syracuse?

Merriam-Webster's Dictionary defines *set in stone* as "permanent . . . not able to be changed." By the time he was seven years old, Henry Keck's life was set in glass.

In 1873, Keck was born in Geissen, Germany. His father, a woodworker and cabinet maker, imparted a dedication to craft and quality to young Henry. Emigrating to the US with his family, at age seven, Keck was apprenticed to Louis Comfort Tiffany, the legendary pioneer of stained-glass techniques whose reputation coined the phrase "Tiffany glass." Working in Tiffany's stained-glass workshops, Keck learned glass cutting and glazing, skills that formed the foundation of what was to come. He returned to Germany in 1895 to attend the Royal Academy School of Industrial Art in Munich, studying the art of glass design and glass painting.

HENRY KECK STAINED GLASS STUDIO

WHAT: A master designer's renowned windows

WHERE: In Syracuse homes and churches nationwide

COST: Free

PRO TIP: The Onondaga Historical Association has put together a detailed exhibit, The Colors of Keck, including drawings of his designs and photography.

Yet back in the States, employment as a designer was hard to find. He worked in Chicago and New York, and came upstate as a designer for Rochester's Pike Stained Glass Studio in 1909. Within four years, he moved to Syracuse to strike out on his own, founding the city's first art glass studio. Residential Arts and Crafts architecture had seen explosive growth in Syracuse thanks to architect Ward Wellington Ward, and once the Keck Stained Glass Studio opened, Ward used Keck's glass exclusively in the homes he designed. Keck's style differed from traditional

Examples of Keck's commercial and residential work.

stained glass design and reflected the influence of Arts and Crafts with small landscapes, careful composition, bright pure colors, and thick leaded outlines.

While the Syracuse houses were a significant portion of his business, Keck gained prominence as a designer of church windows. The naturalism of his human figures and the variety of emotion captured in the glass paintings earned the studio commissions nationwide, cementing his legacy.

After Keck's death in 1956, master stained glass artist Stanley Worden ran the studio for 18 years, maintaining the same level of craftsmanship that Keck was known for.

STRONG SMELL OF SUCCESS

What was that "fragrance" coming out of Bristol all those years ago?

Up until 2004, in the Syracuse neighborhoods surrounding Bristol Myers Squibb in East Syracuse, residents had a saying for those evenings in which the breeze carried a familiar but malodorous scent: "They're making penicillin tonight." For 60 years, as much as 70 percent of what was once the world's most widely used antibiotic was produced at the Thompson Road facility.

Back in 1943 Bristol-Myers came to Syracuse, buying Cheplin Laboratories, which employed just 40 workers. They obtained government sponsorship to build a $1.25-million plant, and Lee Bristol, VP of Bristol-Myers, dedicated the cornerstone of the new facility, saying, "As one who was born in this city, I take special pride in the fact that penicillin, the wonder drug of modern science, is to be made here." The new plant was one of the three largest of its kind in the US.

As the world's first mass-produced drug capable of clearing a bacterial infection, in World War II, penicillin was a critical weapon in the treatment arsenal of modern medicine. The new antibiotic was so effective at eradicating battlefield wound infections, pneumonia, and other bacterial infections, it was

PENICILLIN AT BRISTOL MYERS SQUIBB

WHAT: The wonder drug of modern science

WHERE: 6000 Thompson Road, East Syracuse

COST: Free to drive by, but the original 1943 building and others have been torn down

PRO TIP: While no tours are available, Lotte Biologics, which bought the plant in January 2023 for $160 million, intends to add 50-70 workers, so that's one way in.

A view of the former Bristol campus.

estimated that the mortality rate was reduced by 12–15 percent through the use of penicillin alone.

The East Syracuse facility grew during and after the war years. At the start of the 1950s, 800 workers were spread out across a campus of nine major buildings.

Bristol-Myers continued as a leading penicillin producer, but competition from other manufacturers increased. In 1989, Bristol-Myers merged with Squibb, and, in 2004, the company ended penicillin production in East Syracuse. Though the decision closed the book on the "Penicillin Era," area residents—now free of the fermentation odor that resulted from penicillin manufacturing—could finally breathe a sweet sigh of relief.

Though production figures were said to be classified as a military secret, by 1950, the East Syracuse plant was regarded as the world's largest producer of penicillin.

MORE THAN GOOD BONES

Is it true there's a street where the houses won't burn?

Though Syracuse is thousands of miles away from the wildfires that routinely ravage California, a century ago, Syracuse architect Paul Hueber designed houses anticipating this danger. At least nine of them still stand in Eastwood on a street called Shotwell Park. The outward appearance of each home remains deceptive. The unsuspecting buyers, taken in by the houses' charm, distinctive character, and strong curb appeal, may not realize what they're really buying into. Good bones are the least of it. These houses are fireproof.

According to architectural historian Samuel D. Gruber, during World War I, Hueber served in the navy helping to design ships made of concrete. The building techniques he learned were useful when he returned to civilian life in Syracuse. Working with his brothers who ran the family construction business, he designed and built cast-in-place concrete homes in and around Shotwell Park.

Earlier in 1920, he had submitted an application to the US Patent Office for his "Concrete Building Form." In his 6,000-word filing, he described his invention of "temporary forms for concrete building structures and . . . the method of erecting the[m]." Assembled in place on a building site, they'd be poured and filled with concrete, then "easily and systematically removed and reused in the construction of other concrete buildings." The patent was approved in June 1922.

The Fireproof Houses include 232, 236, 240, 243, 244, 256, 260, 261, and 269 Shotwell Park. As these are private residences and not open to the public, please admire from a distance.

Hueber and one of his concrete homes.
Courtesy of architectural historian Samuel D. Gruber.

In his 1924 paper "Building Fireproof Homes" he argued, "Fireproof homes are by no means a new product. Well-to-do men have been building such homes for years, not because they wanted a cheaper house, but because they wanted the best."

Hueber's best homes have withstood the test of time. Though he went on to build more opulent residential designs, the fireproof houses of Shotwell Park remain a thing of beauty and practicality.

SHOTWELL PARK'S FIREPROOF HOUSES

WHAT: Nine houses constructed of concrete

WHERE: Shotwell Park in the Eastwood neighborhood off James Street

COST: Free

PRO TIP: Follow the Arts and Crafts Society of Central New York on Facebook, which has additional information on these and other Paul Hueber homes.

EN-GULFED BY THE UNKNOWN

Which road is Witch Road?

Chittenango's reputation as a small town has been burnished by the birth of its most famous son, L. Frank Baum, who wrote *The Wonderful Wizard of Oz*. But Syracuse radio station Big Frog 104 observes, "In Chittenango some streets are a dark cousin to the Yellow Brick Road. Several ghost sightings have been reported on one road in particular: Gulf Road."

Gulf Road is a seasonal road winding through isolated woods, starting at the valley hamlet of Mycenae and rising 1.3 miles up Brinkerhoff Hill to reach Salt Springs Road. Its unlucky length is tempered by the presence of Horseshoe Lane, a U-shaped side road with well-kept suburban houses. Once visitors pass that neighborhood, a metal gate long enough to swing across the road closes access in winter.

Rumors keep Gulf Road in the public consciousness as a haunted place. Unlike Gray Road in Minetto whose lurid history is verified by newspaper accounts, Gulf Road's scary reputation is all hearsay.

So here's what they say. According to the New York Haunted Houses website, "Shadow figures have been seen darting across the street, and the specter of a woman often stands on the side of the road." Big Frog 104 elaborates: "Headlights have formed the shadow of a woman in the road, though there has never been a woman standing there."

GULF ROAD IN CHITTENANGO

WHAT: Ghost stories haunt an isolated road.

WHERE: Between NY-5 in Mycenae and Salt Springs Road in Chittenango

COST: Free

PRO TIP: Gulf Road is popular with motorcyclists because of its steep hills and numerous twists and turns.

The road as seen in winter when it's closed due to seasonal conditions.

On the now-inactive Scarycuse forum, pumpkinking writes, "One of the legends . . . is that if you go there at night, you can see bonfires or fairy-fires high up on the wooded hills, and you can hear chanting and crazed laughter. If you leave the road to go into the woods to see the fires, they supposedly go out when you get close, leaving you in the dark, never to find your way back." The forum contributors claim that Gulf Road goes by another name: Witch Road.

Stories are told of burning crosses in the woods. A paranormal investigator named Spear also mentions "odd glowing balls of light . . . and a few white anomalies" in his 2011 blog.

TINY SLOPES

Where's the smallest ski area in the US?

In a city famous for snow, learning how to ski is practically the first line of defense against going stir-crazy during the winter months. If you'd like to learn to ski or snowboard, but you're intimidated by heights, speed, and heck, the whole idea of standing up as you slide downhill, there's a nearby slope designed just for you. It's reportedly the smallest ski area in the US.

For purposes of comparison, here's a look at the other end of the spectrum. The largest ski resort in the country is Park City Mountain with more than 7,300 skiable acres, 348 trails, and 3,200 feet of vertical drop.

Just outside Syracuse is Four Seasons Golf and Ski Center in Fayetteville. Compared to Park City, its 12 skiable acres, 6 trails, and vertical drop (59 feet according to Ski Central, 80 feet at ILovetheFingerLakes.com) are much more manageable for the apprehensive first-timer. In 1995, it had the honor of being named the country's smallest ski slope.

Its size attracts out-of-towners, some of whom have never seen snow before. Owner John Goodfellow points out, "People don't just come from Fayetteville and Manlius or Syracuse. We get them from Albany and people coming up from the South." While visiting a CNY relative, Manchester, New Hampshire WMUR reporter Paula Tracy stopped by and was impressed, calling it "a cute spot. Clean and sunny; a wonderful break outdoors."

They offer a hill for tubing, ski and snowboard lessons, and snow-related programs and camps. Operations Manager Bill

---

If you're not into winter sports, Four Seasons operates soccer and batting cages, miniature golf, and a driving range from April through October.

Inside and out at Four Seasons.

Hane says, "Our core skiers are beginners between five and twelve years old [who] have never skied before." The kids stay busy and have fun—so much fun that Hane says that some parents have been known to "drop them off, and maybe . . . shop for an hour, then come back and pick them up."

FOUR SEASONS GOLF AND SKI

WHAT: America's smallest ski area

WHERE: 8012 E. Genesee Street, Fayetteville

COST: Prices vary for skiing and snow tubing

PRO TIP: The slopes are open December through March and, with snowmaking equipment, average between 80-100 days a season.

THE DARLING OF STRATHMORE AND SEDGWICK

What Syracuse architect is known for his stunning homes?

If you believe a thing of beauty is a joy forever, then you have 78 opportunities to live a joyous life inside a Syracuse residence designed by Ward Wellington Ward. Ward is to Syracuse what Frank Lloyd Wright is to the rest of America—an architect whose name is uttered in tones of admiration and respect, and whose houses are usually treated with reverence by their owners. Some are quaint and picturesque, others are elegant and stately, but all are endowed with those details of thoughtful craftsmanship that distinguish a Ward home from others in their respective neighborhoods.

Primarily a designer of single-family homes, Ward moved to Syracuse in 1908 and practiced here until 1926, when illness ended his career. Though a variety of styles are represented in his design portfolio, he's best known for his Arts and Crafts homes. Among the Ward Wellington Ward residence designs in Syracuse are Tudor Revival, English Cottage, California Bungalow, Swiss Chalet, Colonial Revival, Dutch Colonial, Italian Renaissance,

WARD WELLINGTON WARD HOUSES

WHAT: The residential legacy of Syracuse's premier architect

WHERE: Across Syracuse, especially Strathmore and Sedgwick

COST: Not cheap

PRO TIP: Don't buy a Ward house and neglect it. The Preservation Association of CNY is not above shaming owners by photographing deterioration, naming the address, and publishing photos online.

The one-of-a-kind aspect of a Ward Wellington Ward home adds to its appeal.

and Prairie houses. While his homes are scattered throughout the city, they are concentrated in the neighborhoods of Strathmore, Scottholm, Berkeley Park, and Sedgwick Farms—the affluent residential suburbs of their day.

His Arts and Crafts aesthetic had him turning to fine craftsmen to add detailing to homes that remain unequalled. He made extensive use of Henry Mercer's Moravian Tile, using more Mercer tile in his fireplaces than any other architect. When Henry Keck opened his Syracuse stained glass studio in 1913, Ward relied on Keck for residential stained and regular leaded glass windows.

Ward spent only 18 years in Syracuse working as an architect, and at the tail end, he was also designing homes in Rochester. But in that short period of time, he was prolific, designing 250 buildings. More than 120 of those are still standing; two-thirds are in Syracuse.

Twenty-six Ward houses are listed on the National Register of Historic Places. One that wasn't—the old Le Moyne Manor restaurant overlooking Onondaga Lake—was once his private residence.

IT'S THE PITS

What's that stark, foreboding industrial site just off I-481?

The landscape surrounding Syracuse is pockmarked with quarries, some still active, many abandoned. At the eastern edge of the city, Skytop Quarry borders a suburban neighborhood, golf course, and Syracuse University's South Campus (also called Skytop). Visible from I-481 near the Rock Cut Road exit, the quarry is desolate and creepy—a glimpse of a burnt-out dystopian world. Yelp user Nick K. from San Francisco described it as "eerily wonderful," adding, "I used to come here a lot to go mountain biking with friends. The area has single track gravel paths for beginners and an impressive combination of man-made and natural stunts, hills, drops, bridges, and climbs for more advanced riders."

It's an open secret for mountain biking, though it's technically private and posted. Trailforks.com, a crowd-sourced database that provides information on outdoor trail networks, rates it as "one of the best sets of challenging singletrack in the Central NY area. Trails are a combination of tight, wooded singletrack and rocky, sketchy singletrack." They recommend it for mountain biking (47 trails, 21 miles) along with hiking and trail running (42 trails, 19 miles).

It's an "interesting" hike. The website Atlas Obscura says, "The area is extremely barren, but visitors may discover the occasional wrecked/torched car, 'art installation' (i.e., doll heads lined up on a log), or remnants of a fire pit and/or party. The emptiness and decay [tend] to spook visitors." Syracuse *Post-*

While it's possible to enter from Syracuse University to the west or Old Stonehouse Road to the east, you may be ticketed for parking. Police frequently patrol the area.

A wonderland of creative decay.

Standard reporter Rick Moriarty echoed this, comparing Skytop's many tumbledown buildings to "a ghost town, a Roman [ruin,] and an art park," the latter due to years of "graffiti artists hav[ing] . . . a field day with the site. They have painted over nearly every square inch of the abandoned structures." If all this strangeness tempts you to visit, don't go alone.

SKYTOP QUARRY

WHAT: An abandoned pit with trails

WHERE: Enter from Skytop Parking Lot, 640 Skytop Road, or Old Stonehouse Road, Jamesville.

COST: Free

PRO TIP: The easier mountain biking trails are near Old Stonehouse Road, intermediate trails are by Skytop Lot, and the hardest trails circle the edge of the quarry.

A RIVER RUNS THROUGH IT

What's the best way to enjoy Onondaga Creek?

If you want a completely different view of the city, see it by water. Onondaga Creek has gotten more attention with the opening of the initial phase of Creekwalk in 2011, but that's land-based. To really appreciate it, start up the creek with a paddle.

The main tributary of Onondaga Lake, Onondaga Creek's headwaters are 27 miles south in Tully. For city exploration, go by canoe or kayak starting in the Valley. Creek Rats, a grassroots group that's been cleaning up the creek since 2001, recommends launching at Kelley Brother's Park on Dorwin Avenue and paddling to Ollie's Point in Franklin Square. The route will take you underneath 33 different bridges, and "at Ollie's Point you'll find a well-worn pathway between the Creekwalk and a flat section of shoreline where the creek is naturally shallow . . . an easy exit from your canoe or kayak back to land, and easy access for vehicles to pick up boats."

One person who's tried the morning commute by water is Jason Driscoll. From his Valley home bordering Onondaga Creek, if he launches his kayak at 6:15 a.m., it takes 80 minutes to get to the Inner Harbor and his job on Spencer Street. He's seen a mother duck and ducklings, a family of raccoons, but no humans on the water: "You can see people on the bridges, but I don't think anyone thinks to look down."

ONONDAGA CREEK AND CREEK RATS

WHAT: A volunteer group maintains the city's primary waterway.

WHERE: The length of Onondaga Creek through Syracuse

COST: Free

PRO TIP: At Creekrats.org, they've got everything you need to get started. Click "Enjoy Onondaga Creek," and then click "Boat Safety for Onondaga Creek" for all the details.

Going with the flow near Franklin Square.

Creek Rats know why. Cofounders Steve Seleway and Bob Graham described Onondaga Creek as a water dump before the group started its cleanup program; it was so foul-smelling, they had to throw out their clothes. Today, about 20 Creek Rats are involved with ongoing efforts. They organize four to five events every year. Help them out—they're always looking for new volunteers.

Creek Rats have removed bicycles, tires, guns, street signs, shopping carts, and a phone booth, but four submerged safes and an ATM still sit there, too heavy to budge.

ARE YOU MY MUMMY?

How did Cazenovia end up with a mummy museum in its library?

Libraries typically run book sales as fundraisers. When Cazenovia showed off its authentic Egyptian mummy, after expenses, they raised $26.40.

The mummy was an 1894 gift from the library's biggest benefactor, Robert James Hubbard. A Utica native, Hubbard prospered at a New York City brokerage firm, so in 1875, after he settled in his wife's hometown of Cazenovia, he had the means to help the community. When the public library outgrew its rented space, he bought them a house in 1890 and proposed "gathering and preserving objects of art, curios, and papers of historic value, and . . . local interest."

Hubbard meant what he said. In 1894, he and his son Robert F. embarked on a 10-month grand tour of Europe—the custom of the wealthy back then. It wasn't purely for fun—he had an ulterior motive. The idea of a *wunderkammer*, or cabinet of curiosities, was a popular concept, and Western fascination with the lore and objects of Ancient Egypt had created Egyptomania among the public. Hubbard's Europe and North Africa journeys included some months in Egypt and exploration of the Nile.

At the time, the Egyptian government supported the sale of antiquities, and

Hubbard's Egyptian collection includes Hen, the "lady" mummy, and other artifacts, but that's just one of eight extraordinary collections on display covering history, nature, culture, and art—a must-see.

Outside Central New York's most unique library.

CAZENOVIA LIBRARY'S MUMMY MUSEUM

WHAT: Artifacts from an 1894 grand tour

WHERE: 100 Albany Street, Cazenovia

COST: Free for self-guided tours

PRO TIP: For a minimum of $20 for groups of fewer than 10 people, 45-minute tours of the "Cabinet of Curiosities" or "The Egyptian Program" can be arranged with the library.

Hubbard literally went shopping. In his penciled diary entry dated Friday, March 9, 1894, he wrote, "We went . . . to look at some mummies then—finding something . . . for our Caz Library." Upon his return with his prize acquisition, the Mummy Tea was held in 1894.

Hubbard enjoyed lecturing and educating the community and was playful about it. A set of notes dated 1902 served as the basis for his talks: "In introducing you to the Mummy before us, I must first inform you that it is a Lady and I can hear your natural question, 'How old is she?' . . . Ladies are reluctant to give their ages."

HEAVEN ON EARTH

Who is the little-known millionaire who funded the abolitionist movement?

Everyone knows software genius Bill Gates who donated $94 million of Microsoft stock in 1994 to launch his charitable foundation. But few have heard of millionaire abolitionist Gerrit Smith who, 150 years before Gates, spent his personal fortune to free enslaved people and to fight slavery. By the time of his death, he'd donated approximately $8 million, which, by today's measure of relative wealth, equals $2.78 billion.

Smith judiciously increased what he'd inherited from his father, a partner of John Jacob Astor first in the fur trade, later in land speculation. Though Smith had wanted to be a lawyer, after his mother died, he bought his father's business for $225,000 and eventually ended up owning three-quarters of a million acres of land.

Smith built his empire–and gave it all away–inside a trim red brick building, the Land Office on his estate in tiny Peterboro. There he worked 15/6/55—up to 15 hours a day, 6 days a week, for 55 years. His antislavery efforts turned quiet Peterboro into a major Underground Railroad station and possibly the safest haven on earth. It was said, "There are yet two places where slaveholders cannot come, Heaven and Peterboro." Among others, Harriet Tubman, Frederick Douglass, William Lloyd Garrison, and John Brown

PETERBORO AND GERRIT SMITH

WHAT: Home to the Gerrit Smith Estate and the National Abolition Hall of Fame and Museum

WHERE: The Estate is at 5304 Oxbow Road and the Hall of Fame is at 5525 Pleasant Valley Road, Peterboro.

COST: Admission is $5 at each location.

PRO TIP: While you can view the exterior exhibits dawn to dusk all year round, visit when the buildings are open on weekend afternoons June-August.

Peterboro is well worth a day trip, especially in summer.

came to Smith's Land Office, the de facto center of the abolitionist movement, for financial and intellectual support.

Smith's *think globally, act locally* approach may be why he's relatively unknown today. According to Norman K. Dann, PhD, author of nine books on Peterboro, "all his effort did not bring Smith national recognition...because his successes were accomplished . . . at his own village, town, and county first"; he did so believing "that local examples of success would become influential models for state and national social change."

Today, the Land Office of the Gerrit Smith Estate is a National Historic Landmark, and Peterboro is home to the National Abolition Hall of Fame and Museum.

RESISTANCE IN BLACK AND WHITE

What are the events of the Jerry Rescue?

If you've seen *12 Years a Slave*, which won the 2013 Academy Award for Best Picture, then you understand the brutal impact of the Fugitive Slave Acts of 1793 and 1850, which allowed the "hunting" of suspected runaways in free states, often resulting in free black individuals being captured and sold into slavery.

This is what happened to William "Jerry" Henry, a previously enslaved man from Missouri who'd been living in Syracuse since 1843, working as a cabinet and barrel maker. On October 1, 1851, he was arrested at work and charged as a fugitive slave. He was taken to the southeast corner of Clinton and Water Streets for a hearing. Fortuitously, the antislavery Liberty Party was holding its New York State Convention at a nearby church. When they heard of the arrest, they attempted that afternoon to free Henry, who escaped but was again apprehended. This time, he was moved to the police station for greater security.

That evening, a more organized rescue was led by two local ministers, Rev. Jermain Wesley Loguen who served the Methodist community, and Rev. Samuel J. May, a Unitarian; Loguen, previously enslaved himself, had come to Syracuse from Tennessee in 1841. Peterboro abolitionist Gerrit Smith was also instrumental in the planning.

A crowd numbering in the thousands gathered. At 8:30 p.m., a battering ram was brought out to break down the door of the jail, and rescuers both Black and White helped free Henry. He was

---

The bronze figures in the Clinton Square *Jerry Rescue* monument depict William "Jerry" Henry's October 1, 1851, escape, aided by Rev. Jermaine Loguen and Rev. Samuel May.

hidden in the city for a few days, then taken by wagon to Oswego, where he crossed Lake Ontario to freedom in Kingston, Ontario, Canada.

Twelve Black citizens—Loguen and 11 others—were among the 27 indicted for the rescue. A Black man, Enoch Reed, was the only person convicted, but died before he could appeal.

THE *JERRY RESCUE* MONUMENT

WHAT: A tribute to the 1851 liberation of a free Black man

WHERE: South Clinton Street south of Erie Boulevard West

COST: Free

PRO TIP: Designed by sculptor Sharon BuMann, the bronze, brick, and concrete monument was erected in 1990. On the back side, a marker explains the symbolic elements.

You'll find the monument in the heart of the city at Clinton Square.

SWEET SPRING OR HAUNTED HOLLOW?

Why do spooky stories surround a serene nature preserve?

Investigate "Whiskey Hollow, Baldwinsville" online, and you'll come away with two completely different impressions of the same place. Let's start with the nature lover's version.

Whiskey Hollow Road zigzags northwest from West Dead Creek Road to Perry Road in Van Buren for approximately 1.4 miles. Partly hard-packed gravel and partly unpaved, the narrow and heavily forested road winds through the Whiskey Hollow Nature Preserve, owned by the Central New York Land Trust. According to CNYHiking.com, "These deep woods provide nesting sites for many bird species and the National Audubon Society has named the Hollow an Important Bird Area. It is a great place to explore." Be aware as you drive that the south side of the road is wet with the creek and seeping water, while the north side is drier with ridges and valleys.

The popular Whiskey Hollow Spring is on CNYLT property and is open to the public. At the Find a Spring website, locals say they've been drinking from it for decades with no ill effects. One comment sums it all up: "[T]he water tastes sweet." Up the hill from the spring, there's a deep cave.

WHISKEY HOLLOW ROAD AND SPRING

WHAT: The urban legends surrounding Whiskey Hollow Nature Preserve

WHERE: Whiskey Hollow Road, Van Buren

COST: Free

PRO TIP: While many drink from the spring with no ill effects, previous testing has come back positive for coliform, a precursor to *E. coli* bacteria, so consuming the water is not recommended.

Despite its name the spring serves up water, not whiskey, with plenty of good hikes nearby.

The horror fan's version of Whiskey Hollow is considerably darker. WeirdUS.com claims the area is home to an evil band of Satan worshippers whose victims, mostly children, wander the road. They note that a child's bloody blanket has been spotted hanging in the trees, and that "racial killings and Satanic sacrifices are rumored to have taken place here."

The urban legends prompted a group of Baldwinsville teens to film *Whiskey Hollow* in 2011. Directed and produced by Matt Lipke, the 90-minute movie had its world premiere at the Palace Theatre in January 2012.

Keep in mind that Whiskey Hollow Road is closed at night, not due to any evil reputation but because it's a twisting road with drop-offs and no guardrails.

CHEAP DEALS ON TEALL

Where's the best place to shop for inexpensive groceries and baked goods?

With supermarket prices shooting through the roof in the post-pandemic years—and gas prices as well—everybody is feeling the heat. Even if you've got a PhD in coupon clipping and a road map of what store has what bargains, driving across Syracuse to get these deals can tank your gas budget. Fortunately, one address can cut your grocery bill in half.

LYNCOURT GROCERY OUTLET AND FREIHOFER'S BAKERY OUTLET

WHAT: Food bargains at two outlet stores: one grocery, one baked goods

WHERE: 2301 Teall Avenue

COST: Cheap, often 50-75 percent off the regular price

PRO TIP: Ask whoever's behind the counter at Freihofer's for the weekly schedule of deals, and bring your own bags to Lyncourt.

Lyncourt Grocery Outlet may be small with just three, maybe stretching-it-to-call-it four aisles, but everything you need is there, including fresh fruits and vegetables, freezer cases, a walk-in cooler, dairy products, fresh and frozen meats, cleaning and paper products, pet food, baked goods, and breads, all at incredibly low prices. Because it's an outlet, products will be nearer to the expiration date than you'll find at Wegmans or Tops, but prices are 50 percent, even 75 percent off what you'd pay at the retail stores.

These are not dollar-store mystery labels but quality brand names: Starbucks, Seattle's Best, Peets, Lavazzo, and Paul de Lima coffees; Ben & Jerry's, Halo Top, Klondike Bars,

Häagen-Dazs, Magnum ice creams, and Talenti gelato; and Godiva, Ferrero Rocher, and Lindt chocolates. It's got a robust spices section and a Greek food aisle, and many items are food service–sized for even bigger savings. Open since May 2014, it's surprising that so few people know about it.

Next door is Freihofer's Bakery Outlet, and if you have a sweet tooth, be warned: you *will* overspend. The usual breads are here along with bagels, English muffins, hot dog buns, and hamburger rolls—all ridiculously cheap. Cookies and sweets are deeply discounted, with different specials every day of the week and dollar items on Fridays. Plus, they have chips and snacks, not as deeply discounted, but still well priced. Don't count calories here.

Hidden in Lyncourt is a serious scrimper's salvation, the biggest cheapskate secret in Syracuse: two stores, side by side, with prices so low they're practically giving away food.

Don't forget to bring your grocery bags.

DUCK, DUCK, GOOSE

What popular park is a happy place for everyone from toddlers to anglers?

Webster Pond is a child-pleasing place where you can feed the fish and ducks and walk level trails, all within city limits. A favorite for generations of locals, it was once a trash-strewn site this close to becoming a landfill when an energetic volunteer group took it over. Named after its original owner, Revolutionary War veteran Ephraim Webster, it's managed by the Angler's Association of Onondaga under a long-term lease with the city of Syracuse.

With a timber-reinforced edge and gravel underfoot, the pond is accessible to wheelchairs. So is the short .6-mile trail around Webster Pond.

The pond is available year-round, with operating hours from approximately 9 a.m. to 9 p.m., and volunteers who open the park for visitors. The Anglers Association of Onondaga, assisted by Friends of Wildlife, do the physical work of maintenance, feed the birds 200 pounds of corn every day, and fundraise to keep the pond operating, so donations are appreciated. They'll also teach your device-addicted offspring to put down the gamepad and pick up a fishing pole—their affordable Junior Fishing Program is for ages 7-15.

A Forever Wild Nature Conservation Area, it's had its share of feathered inhabitants: more than two dozen varieties of ducks; four kinds of geese; swans, cormorants, Great Blue herons, kingfishers, bald eagles, seagulls, purple martens, and pigeons.

WEBSTER POND

WHAT: A 95-acre pond/nature sanctuary for fish and wildlife

WHERE: 2004 Valley Drive

COST: Free, but donations are appreciated

PRO TIP: You can give the waterfowl lettuce from home, and feed corn is available for purchase, but don't bring bread, crackers, or baked goods—it'll make them sick.

Webster Pond is literally for the birds—and those who appreciate fowl friends.

And don't forget the mute swan. An impressive assortment of other animals have also been spotted: deer, foxes, minks, raccoons, squirrels, woodchucks, opossums, and three kinds of turtles—box, snapping, and yellow sliders. Photos of more than 50 kinds of critters spotted at Webster Pond are on their website. Start your own checklist, and see how many you can spot.

For its volunteers, Webster Pond is a true labor of love, especially for manager Chad Norton. He's been volunteering there for more than 25 years, beginning when he was 10.

UNIQUE AND FAR AWAY FROM IT ALL

What's a nice hike that has water, woods, views, and full accessibility?

Launch every type of adventure from within this Department of Environmental Conservation–managed state forest. Across 1,483 acres, you'll find woods, wetlands, water features, and trails ideal for hiking in the summer, and perfect for snowshoeing and cross-county skiing in the winter. It's an accessible park for those with mobility issues, featuring a 2,000-foot-long boardwalk and a fishing pier. Both overlook a serene pond that feels far away from it all. If you're not afraid to tackle some steep spots, you can summit Jones Hill and see practically forever from a cleared area popular with hang gliders.

A unique area, according to the state DEC, is "land owned by the state that was acquired due to its special natural beauty, wilderness character, or for its geological, ecological or historical significance." Included are "rare plant life and scarce animal habitats."

Many of those features are present in Labrador Hollow, starting with the landscape itself. A narrow glacial valley running north to south, it was dug out by the same glaciers that created the Finger Lakes. Only a half-mile wide, the valley's steep walls rise up several hundred feet, making it both picturesque and an ecological treasure.

Turkey, ruffed grouse, woodcock, and other waterfowl call Labrador Hollow home. Look for an osprey nesting platform on the pond's west side. More than 107 different bird species have been spotted.

The view from Jones Hill and down in the Hollow.

LABRADOR HOLLOW UNIQUE AREA

WHAT: A glacial valley far away from it all

WHERE: Route 91 to Labrador Crossroad—watch for signs

COST: Free

PRO TIP: While all trails are open all year round, Skyline Trail can be tricky in snow and mud season.

Labrador Pond is shallow at only four feet deep with an accessible dock/boat launch for canoes and kayaks on the western shoreline. The boardwalk loop at the northern tip has several benches along its stretch. Southeast of the pond, Tinker Falls can be reached by a flat gravel path, also accessible, and it's only a quarter-mile to the 50-foot falls from the parking lot/trailhead. A short distance from that trailhead, the Skyline Trail will take you up Jones Hill, the eastern ridge of the valley, to the hang glider launch spot, for an up-and-back hike of three miles.

ROADS TO NOWHERE

Why are there unmarked exits from I-481 and I-690?

As a kid, you were scared silly by "haunted" roads. As an adult, maybe you avoid them at night. But the true "ghost" roadways of our transportation system go largely unremarked. In Syracuse, the "ghost ramps" of the Butternut Interchange are highway ramps inaccessible to traffic because they've been taken out of use.

At the eastern terminus of Interstate 690, at its intersection with Interstate 481, four ghost ramps are clearly visible on aerial maps. Two are on-ramps, two are off-ramps, and all four connect to active highways. However, striping, signage, and other tricks fool you into not noticing them.

Ghost Ramp #1 enters 690 West just as it splits from 481. Take 481 North and turn onto Exit 4—West 690. Look for a West 690 shield on the right. The ghost ramp enters there through an underpass formed by northbound 481. Ghost Ramp #2 enters 481 North just past Exit 4 after the overpass; when the right-hand guardrail ends, Ghost Ramp #2 creeps in. Ghost Ramp #3 is on 481 South, just beyond the underpass formed by 690 East turning onto 481 South; an unmarked road just off the far left lane, it's flanked by two DO NOT ENTER signs.

Ghost Ramp #4 is obvious. Take 690 East to its end. The far-left EXIT ONLY lane leads to North 481 to 90 Thruway; stay

BUTTERNUT INTERCHANGE GHOST RAMPS

WHAT: Roads that go nowhere from two interstate highways

WHERE: Along I-481 North, I-481 South, I-690 West, and I-690 East

COST: Free

PRO TIP: All four ghost ramps lead to the New York Department of Transportation facility at 5831 Butternut Drive. Don't drive these ghost ramps for kicks—they'll see you coming.

Once you see them, you can't unsee them. . . . but don't follow them unless you want a ticket.

on the double-lane highway heading to 481 South DeWitt. There, the far left shoulder becomes as wide as the highway itself. Striped with forbidding yellow paint, that's the long offramp to Ghost Ramp #4 on the left.

These ramps were originally built for a proposed highway to the eastern suburbs that never materialized. EmpireStateRoads.com notes, "Remarkably, all of the unused ramps and overpasses are visible . . . that would have provided the northbound-to-eastbound connection."

In 1965, the Syracuse *Post-Standard* described a Fayetteville Bypass proposal "to avoid complete clogging of traffic between Lyndon and DeWitt." That problem remains, although the ghost ramps anticipated that bypass.

SOURCES

Misfortune's Beauty

Bone, James. *The Curse of Beauty: The Scandalous and Tragic Life of Audrey Munson, America's First Supermodel.* New York: Regan Arts, 2016; https://www.nytimes.com/2022/12/15/obituaries/audrey-munson-overlooked.html; https://timesmachine.nytimes.com/timesmachine/1922/05/28/109336933.html?pageNumber=2; https://www.allure.com/story/audrey-munson-supermodel-story; https://www.centralparknyc.org/locations/pulitzer-fountain; https://ephemeralnewyork.wordpress.com/tag/civic-fame-statue/; https://www.wgpfoundation.org/historic-markers/audrey-munson/; https://www.democratandchronicle.com/story/lifestyle/2016/04/29/americas-first-nude-supermodel-born-rochester/83656636/.

Eight Is Enough

https://www.iloveny.com/listing/octagon-house-of-camillus/43699/; https://cnycentral.com/news/your-town/your-town-camillus-octagon-house; https://daily.jstor.org/a-phrenologists-dream-of-an-octagon-house/; http://www.yrbook.com/octagon/; https://www.buffaloah.com/a/NEWST/main/145/index.html; https://www.waymarking.com/waymarks/wm4EG2_Wilcox_Octagon_House_Camillus_New_York.

Man Cave Manor

https://timesmachine.nytimes.com/timesmachine/1978/05/06/110943227.html?pageNumber=26; https://www.oswegocountynewsnow.com/news/after-covid-delay-new-casey-s-cottage-ready-to-shine-as-one-of-areas-hidden/article_8b3c6fea-add9-11eb-ac52-a3e719b7a115.html; https://oswegocountytoday.com/oswego-tourism/colorful-history-unveiled/; http://artsandnatureinoswego.blogspot.com/2009/08/; http://mexicopointpark.com/wp/?page_id=28.

Best of the Rest

https://www.youtube.com/watch?v=vh-K0pGoo3zA; https://www.youtube.com/watch?v=R6eX9YV_SuY; https://southerncalls.com/article/the-marsellus-casket-company/#open-overlay; https://myundertaking.wordpress.com/2008/08/01/the-marsellus-masterpiece/; https://apnews.com/article/a1607ad70f5f1d835f5031d606b471bc; https://blog.sullivanfuneraldirectors.com/two-caskets-historic-and-patriotic/; https://www.nytimes.com/2003/03/28/nyregion/coffin-maker-in-syracuse-is-shut-down-315-jobs-lost.html; https://www.syracuse.com/opinion/2010/10/john_marsellus_fondly_remember.html; https://www.syracuse.com/news/2014/08/one_marsellus_casket_building_will_be_torn_down_another_redeveloped.html; https://www.syracuse.com/news/2013/12/former_marsellus_casket_factory_to_become_new_home_of_rural_metro_ambulance.html; https://hocpa.org/wp-content/uploads/2020/02/2016-spring.pdf.

Accidental Casket of Camelot

https://www.syracuse.com/opinion/2010/10/john_marsellus_fondly_remember.html; https://www.cfsaa.org/notable-individuals-and-their-marsellus-caskets/; https://www.syracuse.com/news/2010/09/marsellus_casket_made_fine_woo.html; https://www.syracuse.com/living/2015/11/this_week_in_history_-_kennedy_casket_a_product_of_syracuse.html; https://anthonybergen.medium.com/burial-at-sea-the-odyssey-of-jfks-original-casket-8c458b758c64; http://www.pinkpillbox.com/index.php/9-historical-record.

Ruler of The Palace

Case, Dick. *Remembering Syracuse.* Charleston, SC: History Press, 2013; https://obits.syracuse.com/us/obituaries/syracuse/name/frances-dibella-obituary?id=29736133; https://www.palaceonjames.com.

Wooden It Be Nice

https://library.syracuse.edu/digital/guides/s/syroco.htm; https://library.syracuse.edu/blog/a-century-of-syroco/; https://www.tiktok.com/tag/syroco; https://www.etsy.com/search?q=syroco&ref=search_bar; https://www.ebay.com/sch/i.html?_from=R40&_trksid=p2499334.m570.l1313&_nkw=-Syroco&_sacat=0; https://www.syracuse.com/news/2007/06/syroco_plant_closes_for_good_t.html; https://www.syracuse.com/business-news/2017/10/redevelopment_plan_in_the_works_for_abandoned_syracuse_area_factory_photos.html.

Haunted or Punk'd?

https://www.southcoasttoday.com/story/lifestyle/2000/10/25/woman-says-she-invented-community/50475331007/; https://www.wgpfoundation.org/historic-markers/thirteen-curves/; http://www.weirdus.com/states/new_york/road_less_traveled/bloody_bride_of_13_curves/index.php; https://www.onlyinyourstate.com/new-york/thirteen-curves-ny/.

Off the Rails

https://www.syracuse.com/living/2015/03/central_new_york_spaces_martisco_station.html; https://www.newyorkbyrail.com/local-guide/martisco-station-museum/; https://shiningtimestation.fandom.com/wiki/Mr._Conductor.

The Greatest Showman

Howard, Ryan. *Punch and Judy in 19th Century America: A History and Biographical Dictionary.* Jefferson, NC: McFarland, March 2013; https://www.crookedlakereview.com/articles/67_100/91oct1995/91harris.html; https://www.classic.circushistory.org/History/BriefS.htm; https://www.lifeinthefingerlakes.com/homers-sig-sautelle/; http://newyorkhistoryreviewarticles.blogspot.com/2020/04/the-trials-and-tribulations-of-homers.html; https://www.google.com/books/edition/Punch_and_Judy_in_19th_Century_America/GjJjYwNPCfEC?hl=en&gbpv=1&dq=curtis+harris+sig+sautelle&pg=PA207&printsec=frontcover; https://www.cnyhistory.org/2014/10/sig-sautelle-cat-act/.

Under the Big Top

https://pacny.net/cortland-county-sig-sautelle-circus-house/; https://cortlandvoice.com/2018/10/24/homers-circus-house-placed-on-list-of-historic-properties/; http://newyorkhistoryreviewarticles.blogspot.com/2020/04/the-trials-and-tribulations-of-homers.html; https://www.circusesandsideshows.com/owners/sigsautelle.html; https://www.yumpu.com/en/document/read/4747840/hobby-bandwagon-august-1948-vol-3-no-7-circus-historical-; https://www.cnyhistory.org/2014/10/sig-sautelle-cat-act/; https://www.elephant.se/location2.php?location_id=3598.

Too Cool for School

https://www.nytimes.com/2021/11/21/business/media/american-high-teen-comedies-movies.html; https://deadline.com/2017/07/jeremy-garelick-mickey-liddell-ld-entertainment-american-high-film-comedies-1202136667/; https://americanhigh.com/about-us/.

How Sweet It Was

https://www.oswegocountynewsnow.com/news/new-book-charts-history-of-fulton-nestle-factory/article_a61be144-c040-11e8-82e0-936958a667ba.html; https://www.syracuse.com/business-news/2016/03/birthplace_of_the_nestle_crunch_gets_crunched_in_fulton.html; https://www.nytimes.com/2003/05/02/nyregion/when-the-chocolate-melted-nestle-factory-closing-leaves-town-reeling.html.

The (Hairy) Eagle Has Landed

http://www.thehistoryblog.com/archives/62327; https://www.smithsonianmag.com/history/this-civil-warera-eagle-sculpture-was-made-out-of-abraham-lincolns-hair-180978740/; https://www.syracuse.com/entertainment/2019/07/abraham-lincolns-hair-preserved-in-priceless-syracuse-sculpture-video.html; https://www.loc.gov/resource/sn83030313/1864-04-04/ed-1/?sp=3&r=0.333,1.193,0.168,0.081,0; https://www.cnyhistory.org/2020/04/abraham-lincolns-hair-picture/.

The Original Iron Man

Green, Archie. *Tin Men.* Champaign, IL: University of Illinois Press, 2002; https://www.google.com/books/edition/Tin_Men/pwlXK9ZPsXkC?hl=e; https://groups.google.com/g/alt.culture.ny-upstate/c/SQCMxow2_aM; https://www.cnyhistory.org/2015/12/heaphy-tin-man/.

Minetto's Midnight Ghosts

https://www.syracuse.com/strangecny/2007/11/the_gray_road_ghost.html; https://www.oswegocountynewsnow.com/news/urban-legends-of-oswego-the-ghost-of-gray-road/article_0f9d07da-7941-11ec-b6e5-d7b86e15ffbe.html

A Platform for Commuter Art

https://cnycentral.com/news/local/statues-of-passengers-return-to-restored-train-platform-by-rt690-in-downtown-syracuse; https://www.syracuse.com/news/2016/11/artist_who_created_iconic_train_statues_scarves_arent_part_of_the_art_work_video.html; https://www.syracuse.com/news/2016/01/public_and_sculptor_want_new_york_to_keep_sculptures_on_old_train_platform.html; https://www.syracuse.com/opinion/2010/12/plaster_figures_on_former_trai.html.

The Village That Raised a President

https://www.hamilton.edu/magazine/fall15/the-hill-in-history; https://www.zillow.com/homes/109-Academy-St-Fayetteville,-NY-13066_rb/31744912_zpid/?; https://www.hmdb.org/m.asp?m=96143; https://www.syracuse.com/living/2022/06/the-childhood-home-of-a-former-us-president-is-for-sale-in-fayetteville-photos.html; https://presidentcleveland.org/president-clevelands-biography/president-clevelands-biography-2/; https://archive.nytimes.com; www.nytimes.com/learning/general/onthisday/bday/0318.html.

The Falls Guy

https://nyfalls.com/waterfalls/three-falls-woods/; https://www.madisoncounty.ny.gov/2312/Delphi-Falls-Park; https://www.oneidadispatch.com/2022/07/09/delphi-falls-county-park-set-to-begin-phase-1-improvements/; https://www.syracuse.com/news/2018/01/retired_su_professor_gives_15_million_plus_to_buy_private_cny_waterfalls_land_fo.html; https://www.syracuse.com/news/2018/08/cnys_newest_park_waterfalls_opens_quietly_hosts_wedding.html.

Up on the Roof

https://gizmodo.com/strange-and-gorgeous-houses-built-on-rooftops-1136862204; https://www.roadsideamerica.com/tip/14258; https://nypost.com/2020/02/04/syracuse-factory-with-mysterious-rooftop-house-for-sale/; https://www.syracuse.com/news/2013/08/take_a_tour_of_the_mysterious_house_on_roof_of_old_syracuse_factory.html; https://www.syracuse.com/business/2022/06/construction-starts-on-loft-apartments-at-syracuse-factory-with-house-on-top.html/.

"Cotten Picking" in Syracuse

https://www.syracuse.com/kirst/2012/10/libba_cotten_in_syracuse_her_i.html; https://www.arts.gov/honors/heritage/elizabeth-cotten; https://folkways.si.edu/elizabeth-cotten-master-american-folk/music/article/smithsonian; https://americanhistory.si.edu/collections/search/object/nmah_606741; https://www.syracuse.com/music/2022/05/a-star-after-60-syracuses-elizabeth-libba-cotten-taught-jerry-garcia-pete-seeger-the-meaning-of-folk-music.html; https://www.syracuse.com/cny/2010/02/libbas_legacy_musician_elizabeth_cotten_to_be_honored_with_statue.html; https://www.syracuse.com/entertainment/2022/05/syracuse-folk-legend-libba-cotten-to-be-inducted-into-rock-and-roll-hall-of-fame.html; https://timesmachine.nytimes.com/timesmachine/1987/06/30/issue.html; https://www.syracuse.com/news/2012/06/rev_larry_ellis_advocate_for_n.html.

That Seventies Mall

https://static.wixstatic.com/media/546799_7099eab30bb2466c873682f365cf1dad~mv2.jpg; https://www.newyorkupstate.com/central-ny/2018/01/flashback_big_battle_over_what_to_

name_i-81_in_1958.html; https://static.wixstatic.com/media/546799_47484dfd30bf-40d6ad460e648475be0a~mv2.gif; https://static.wixstatic.com/media/546799_da54d-24d2e6e47c8ae448e1d443fb763~mv2.gif; https://www.syracusenostalgia.com/penn-can-mall; https://www.syracusenewtimes.com/blasts-from-the-past/; https://www.syracuse.com/vintage/2016/04/penn_can_mall_opens_40_years_a.html.

Storm of the Century

https://www.syracuse.com/weather/2018/03/blizzard_of_93_storm_of_the_century.html; https://www.syracuse.com/vintage/2016/03/remembering_the_storm_of_the_c.html; https://www.newyorkupstate.com/weather/2017/03/exactly_24_years_after_blizzard_of_93_central_new_york_prepares_for_15_inches_of.html; https://www.history.com/news/major-blizzards-in-u-s-history; https://cnycentral.com/news/local/watch-nbc3s-hour-long-special-coverage-of-the-blizzard-of-93.

Clarissa Explains It All

https://dailyorange.com/2010/10/playing-dead-inspiring-plays-books-the-landmark-theatre-s-reported-ghost-lives-on-in-memory/; https://eaglenewsonline.com/new/2011/10/25/more-half-dozen-hauntings-detect-ed-syracuse/; https://www.syracuse.com/kirst/2005/10/in_syracuse_the_land-mark_theatre_is_haunted_maybe_even_by_ghosts.html; https://www.syracuse.com/news/2010/09/landmarks_ghostly_pres-ence_to.html; https://www.onlyinyourstate.com/new-york/haunted-theater-ny/; https://www.facebook.com/Landmarktheatre/posts/pfbid0yESn78phF7YFPWuW6j1oWpmzvosjBb-5v16XiqDCHt6PPsqUUMTemRqazJ9eH7B3zl.

Retail Make-Believe

https://www.syracusenostalgia.com/switz-s; https://static.wixstatic.com/media/546799_21974011f74a4b8e96cfdbf8dbaf1f1a~mv2.jpg; https://static.wixstatic.com/media/546799_8d04179d045d45269302e0f-51544cffc~mv2.gif; https://newspaperarchive.com/syracuse-post-standard-jul-30-1993-p-1/.

Lovable Lord of Darkness

https://www.syracuse.com/living/2020/10/halloween-in-the-80s-did-you-visit-oscar-the-monster-at-switzs-photos.html; https://www.syracusenostalgia.com/switz-s; https://static.wixstatic.com/media/546799_4ccd-c1ffdd5a44e593a46df0b1e76328~mv2.gif; https://static.wixstatic.com/media/546799_21974011f74a4b8e96cfdbf8dbaf1f1a~mv2.jpg; https://www.facebook.com/syracusenostalgia/photos/please-share-this-photo-and-help-us-find-oscar/1547732095252886/; https://www.cafepress.com/oscar.

A Sucker Born Every Minute

https://www.history.com/news/the-cardiff-giant-fools-the-nation-145-years-ago https://www.legendsofamerica.com/ny-cardiffgiant/; https://www.smithsonianmag.com/smart-news/cardiff-giant-was-just-big-hoax-180965274/; https://www.bookbrowse.com/expressions/detail/index.cfm/expression_number/212/theres-a-sucker-born-every-minute; https://www.hmdb.org/m.asp?m=40056; https://www.hmdb.org/m.asp?m=40055.

(Almost) The World's Smallest Church

https://spectrumlocalnews.com/nys/watertown/explore-ny/2016/09/7/explore-ny-tiny-church-oneida-madison-county; https://www.uticaod.com/story/news/2011/07/28/tiniest-church-made-to-honor/44831212007/; https://www.roadsideamerica.com/story/2435; https://wanderstarr.com/listing/cross-island-chapel/.

The Magic Key

https://www.youtube.com/watch?v=AoYJjiUIK-Pc; https://surface.syr.edu/cgi/viewcontent.cgi?article=1050&context=libassoc; https://www.syracuse.com/vintage/2017/09/on_this_date_magic_toy_shop_ends_its_run_after_27_years.html; https://www.syracuse.com/news/2008/04/jean_daughtery_play_lady_dead.html.

Signs of the Times

https://www.wgpfoundation.org/history; https://www.wgpfoundation.org/life/bills-story/; https://www.wgpfoundation.org/who-we-are/; https://news.rpi.edu/luwakkey/2421; https://ncwhs.org/news/april-30-is-national-historic-marker-day/.

The Art of Walking

Interview with Laura Reeder on Zoom, February 9, 2023; https://laurakreeder.com/artist/; https://www.syracuse.com/entertainment/2022/01/whats-up-with-those-massive-snow-spirals-at-syracuses-woodland-reservoir.html.

Get Out of the Wayside

https://cnycentral.com/news/local/haunted-cny-mysterious-spirits-haunt-elbridge-pub; https://waysideirishpub.weebly.com/history.html; https://hauntedhistorytrail.com/explore/wayside-irish-pub.

The Hazards of a Company Town

https://www.solvay.com/en/our-company/history/1863-1885; https://www.rihs.org/mssinv/Mss483sg06.htm; https://www.ansac.com/products/about-soda-ash/; https://www.chemeurope.com/en/encyclopedia/Solvay_Process_Company.html; https://www.hmdb.org/m.asp?m=176184.

Bucket List

DeLawyer, Mark W. "The Split Rock Cable Road." Wire Rope News & Sling Technology. June 1988: 14-19; http://major-smolinski.com/READ/BUCKETS.html; https://www.governor.ny.gov/sites/default/files/atoms/files/StateFairAerialGondolaFactSheet.pdf; https://rural-ruin.livejournal.com/170835.html?.

Fire in the Hole

https://eaglenewsonline.com/new/2018/07/16/historic-moment-a-look-back-at-split-rock-explosion/; https://www.localsyr.com/news/local-news/2018-marks-100-years-since-deadly-split-rock-explosion/; https://www.syracuse.com/vintage/2018/06/one_hundred_years_later_remembering_the_split_rock_disaster.html; http://mycentralnewyork.blogspot.com/2017/07/syracuse-ny.html; https://www.newyorkalmanack.com/2018/04/onondaga-historians-marking-split-rock-explosion/; https://ohiomemory.org/digital/collection/p267401coll34/id/8351/; https://briggslibrary.com/content/semet-solvay-company.

Making Marriage Complex

https://www.nytimes.com/1993/10/24/books/complex-marriage-to-say-the-least.html; https://www.nytimes.com/2007/08/03/travel/escapes/03Oneida.html; https://www.oneidacommunity.org; https://www.oneida.com/pages/about-us; https://www.britannica.com/biography/John-Humphrey-Noyes.

The Coney Island of CNY

https://www.hmdb.org/m.asp?m=144419; http://freepages.rootsweb.com/~howardlake/history/amusement7/manhattanbeachupperny.html; https://lpl.org/research/liverpool-ny/photo-collections/onondaga-lake-amusement-parks-and-resorts-of-the-golden-age/; https://www.syracuse.com/empire/2015/07/a_search_for_the_lost_resorts_of_onondaga_lake.html; https://cdm16694.contentdm.oclc.org/digital/collection/livpub01/id/1100/; https://cdm16694.contentdm.oclc.org/digital/collection/livpub01/id/1753; https://www.reddit.com/r/Syracuse/comments/sooels/danforth_salt_pool_it_was_constructed_for/; https://cdm16694.contentdm.oclc.org/digital/collection/livpub01/id/1725/rec/1; https://cdm16694.contentdm.oclc.org/digital/collection/srr_sph/id/19/rec/3; http://syracusebaseballhistory.blogspot.com/2012/01/history-1-babe-ruth-in-syracuse.html; http://freepages.rootsweb.com/~howardlake/history/amusement7/manhattanbeachupperny.html.

Planting Hope Amid Grief

Sternberg, Bill. "Bereaved Parents Help One Another." Syracuse *Post-Standard.* March 27, 1979; Roberts, Ellen. "Garden Will Bloom with Remembrance." Syracuse *Post-Standard.* May 21, 1992; Brooks, Wendy. "Butterfly Garden Serves Community." Syracuse *Post-Standard,* June 19, 2003; https://www.localsyr.com/community/tell-me-something-good/tell-me-something-good-therese-schoeneck-creator-of-hope-for-bereaved/; https://hopeforbereaved.com.

When the Wall Came Tumbling Down

https://www.syracuse.com/entertainment/2014/11/berlin_wall_syracuse_most.html; https://www.waer.org/arts-culture/2015-08-11/peace-garden-behind-the-most-now-showcases-piece-of-german-history; https://www.wrvo.org/regional-coverage/2014-11-12/piece-of-history-hides-out-in-syracuses-armory-square.

Death's a Beach

https://www.cnyhomepage.com/news/syfy-tv-show-ghost-hunters-episode-will-feature-sylvan-beach/; https://www.syfy.com/ghost-hunters/season-9/blogs/episode-recap-scream-park; https://www.syracuse.com/entertainment/2013/02/ghost_hunters_sylvan_beach_syfy_tv_scream_park.html; https://www.syracuse.com/news/2012/09/tvs_ghost_hunters_find_signifi.html; https://cnyradio.com/2013/02/20/ghost-hunters-visit-sylvan-beach-episode-airs-on-syfy-next-week/; https://bigfrog104.com/sylvan-beach-amusement-park-haunted-ghosts/.

Grand Canyon of Syracuse

https://www.waer.org/community/2017-06-19/syracuse-parks-dept-at-100-the-grand-canyon-of-syracuse-hides-in-plain-sight-in-elmwood-park; http://www.syrgov.net/parks/elmwoodPark.html; https://www.syracuse.com/kirst/2006/03/the_international_tolkien_read.html; https://iroquoistu.org/area-streams/furnance-brook/index.html; https://fishonondagacounty.com/about-the-fishing/bodies-of-water/furnace-brook/; https://www.syracuse.com/opinion/2012/03/with_a_little_help_two_old_syr.html.

Arts Take Flight

https://spectrumlocalnews.com/nys/central-ny/news/2018/12/26/airport-museum-welcomes-travelers; http://exhibitsandmore.com/project/syracuse-airport-aviation-museum/; https://pawsofcny.org/pets-easing-travelers/; https://syrairport.org/airport-guide/; https://www.wrvo.org/2022-12-16/syracuse-airports-reading-runway-provides-new-option-to-traveling-families; https://cnycentral.com/news/local/syracuse-airport-announces-syr-reading-runway; https://syrairport.org/syr-unveils-childrens-library-with-ocpl/.

DIY House of Spirits

Zimmer, Melanie. *Curiosities of Central New York.* Charleston, SC: History Press, 2012; https://wisdom-magazine.com/Article.aspx/2140/; https://www.syracuse.com/news/2011/11/sudden_cash_offer_ends_groups.html; https://pacny.net/madison-county-spirit-house-browns-hall/; https://www.syracuse.com/at-home/2009/08/house_of_the_week_georgetowns.html; https://www.ovcs.org/Downloads/Georgetown_-_The_Spirit_House.pdf; https://www.historic-structures.com/ny/georgetown/spirit_house.php; https://www.federalregister.gov/documents/2006/03/03/E6-2999/national-register-of-historic-places-notification-of-pending-nominations-and-related-actions.

Syracuse's Place at the Table

http://waywiser.fas.harvard.edu/people/9265/pass-and-seymour-inc;jsessionid=B8902CC81EAEAC1D1ACCA7069D298B1A; http://64.111.124.182/History/SyracuseChinaHistory.htm; https://www.cnyhistory.org/2017/01/syracuse-china/; http://campusarch.msu.edu/?p=3944; http://www.collectics.com/education_syracuse.html; https://www.cnyhistory.org/explore/collections-2/ https://major-smolinski.com/TALES/PASSEYMOUR.html.

The Dynamic Ceramic Duo

http://waywiser.fas.harvard.edu/people/9265/pass-and-seymour-inc;jsessionid=B8902CC81EAEAC1D1ACCA7069D298B1A; https://www.syracuse.com/living/2022/07/how-syracuse-china-contributed-to-electricitys-growth-in-america.html; https://major-smolinski.com/TALES/PASSEYMOUR.html.

Bomb in a China Shop

https://www.syracuse.com/living/2022/07/how-syracuse-china-contributed-to-electricitys-growth-in-america.html; https://www.cnyhistory.org/2017/01/syracuse-china/; https://www.syracuse.com/opinion/2011/05/syracuse_china_didnt_serve_tea.html; https://onondagacountyparks.com/activity/historic-sites/

Good Vibes Only
https://www.cnyhistory.org/2014/09/ho-tel-syracuse-opens/; https://www.syracuse.com/entertainment/2021/10/the-beatles-almost-reunited-in-syracuse-and-it-started-on-john-lennons-birthday-50-years-ago.html; https://www.syracuse.com/kirst/2005/12/imagine_john_lennon_and_an_alm.html; https://eaglenewsonline.com/new/2011/10/25/more-half-dozen-hauntings-detected-syra-cuse/; http://national-paranormal-society.org/hotel-syracuse/; https://timesmachine.nytimes.com/timesmachine/1984/01/02/149683.ht-ml?pageNumber=26; https://www.cnyhistory.org/hotel-syracuse-tours/; MacMillan, Neil K. *Haunted Onondaga County*. Charleston, SC: History Press, 2015.

What Lies Beneath
https://www.syracuse.com/kirst/2015/11/hotel_syracuse_tunnel_to_oncen-ter_fascinating_relic_but_no_priority.html; "Construct Pedestrian Tunnel." Syracuse *Post-Standard*, June 13, 1967; https://www.facebook.com/plugins/post.php?href=https%3A%2F%2Fwww.facebook.com%2FSyracuseHistory%2Fposts%2Fpf-bid037gSZ8XZY9vpm2hRX9kyaHkT84Pw5DZ-zMPGvvWgiTe5vZik6NzF5gZNgxnru4R5ucl.

Just My Type
https://www.cnyhistory.org/2017/02/lc-smith-brothers-typewriter-co/; https://www.syracuse.com/living/2021/01/at-one-time-half-the-type-writers-in-america-were-made-in-syracuse.html; https://www.referenceforbusiness.com/history2/50/Smith-Corona-Corp.html#ix-zz7qJlGh96p; https://www.syracuse.com/entertainment/2017/04/tom_hanks_bonds_with_onondaga_historical_association_over_shared_love_of_typewri.html.

Gearing Up for the Future
https://www.cnyhistory.org/wp-content/themes/oha/press/2014-11-07-BJ-BLC.pdf; https://www.syracuse.com/kirst/2008/07/vacation_thoughts_vii_hardware.html; https://dailyorange.com/2018/01/syracuses-in-dustrial-past-highlighted-preservation-his-toric-building/; https://www.syracuse.com/kirst/2015/10/the_gear_factory_new_win-dows_bright_sunlight_the_ghost_of_al-bert_kahn.html; https://www.syracuse.com/kirst/2012/08/post_310.html; http://www.coachbuilt.com/des/b/brown/brown.htm; http://wikimapia.org/17887924/Lipe-Machine-Shop.

Lipe of Luxury
https://thecatholicsun.com/under-the-big-tent-sacred-stories-family-tales/; https://www.findagrave.com/memorial/108132901/marjo-rie-stacy; https://www.syracusediocese.org/offices/christ-the-king-retreat-house/; https://ctkretreat.com.

Banking on Franklin
https://www.franklincar.org/index.php; https://www.franklincar.org/about/history/company.html; http://64.111.124.182/History/Industri-alAgeFedSyracuseBoom.htm; https://www.cnyhistory.org/2015/11/franklin-automobile/.

An Inventor, a Doctor, a Soy Candlemaker
Interview with Patti McDermott, February 16, 2023; https://www.cnyhistory.org/video/alexander-t-brown/; https://peoplepill.com/people/alexander-t-brown; https://www.flickr.com/photos/onasill/29261666122; http://www.coachbuilt.com/des/b/brown/brown.htm; https://www.wikiwand.com/en/Alexan-der_Brown_House.

Syracuse's Lost Xanadu
"Cafe Dewitt Opening Tomorrow." *Syracuse Herald*, September 4, 1931; "Receiver Asked for Julian Brown $2,000,000 Holdings." *Syracuse Herald*, November 3, 1931; "Where Submerged Tanks Cause Alarm." *Syracuse Herald*, November 22, 1939; https://www.syracuse.com/living/2022/08/meet-ju-lian-brown-a-wealthy-heir-nightclub-own-er-inventor-and-syracuses-most-investigat-ed-citizen.html; https://www.cnyhistory.org/wp-content/themes/oha/press/GoodLifeCen-tralNY_20150701_B78-B82.pdf.

Inside the Printers' Studio
https://www.boxcarpress.com; https://smockpaper.com/about/; https://apps.carleton.edu/voice/?story_id=1836761&is-sue_id=1836011; https://connectivecorridor.syr.edu/boxcar-press-makes-an-imprint-on-the-connective-corridor/; https://www.syracuse.com/living/2018/09/boxcar_press_turns_20_peek_inside_buzzing_letter-press_studio.html; https://www.syracuse.com/living/2022/11/a-mysterious-machine-in-a-syr-acuse-warehouse-keeps-old-movies-alive-its-the-last-of-its-kind-in-the-world.html; https://delavanstudios.com/shop/holiday-open-stu-dios-2022/.

Death of a Once-Happy Valley
https://sites.rootsweb.com/~nyoswego/towns/williamstown/Fraicheur.html; https://michaelk-leen.com/2017/06/21/happy-valley-ghost-town-oswego-county-new-york/; https://www.newyorkupstate.com/northern-ny/2016/04/rediscovering_happy_valley_ny.html; https://lite987.com/exploring-the-happy-valley-ghost-town-near-syracuse-the-haunts-and-legends-of-new-york/; https://www.dec.ny.gov/outdoor/68691.html.

Surviving the "Fist of God"
Case, Dick. "Delavan Center's Tenants Pull Together." *Syracuse Herald-Journal*, September 17, 1998; https://www.localsyr.com/weather/storm-team-headlines/a-look-back-1998-la-bor-day-storm/; https://www.syracuse.com/news/2018/09/labor_day_storm_1998_20_years_ago_the_fist_of_god_hit_syracuse.html; https://www.weather.gov/bgm/pastSe-vereSeptember071998.

A-Tisket, A-Tasket
https://eaglenewsonline.com/things-to-do/2021/07/20/master-basketmaker-pre-serves-the-style-of-historic-liverpool-weav-ers-workshop-is-aug-14-15/; https://cnycentral.com/news/your-town/willows-a-big-part-of-liverpool-history; http://www.villageofli-verpool.org/village-history.html.

Five Feet from Death

https://www.syracuse.com/news/2011/08/onondaga_lake_story.html; "Airman's Jet Plunges into Onondaga Lake: Vertigo Seen Cause in Young Flier's Death." Syracuse *Post-Standard*, November 27, 1955. https://www.newspapers.com/image/16004462/?terms=Onondaga%20Lake%20Jet%20Crash; "Lt. Kesel's Plane Will Remain at Bottom of Lake." Syracuse *Post-Standard*, November 29, 1955. https://www.newspapers.com/image/16004501/?terms=Onondaga%20Lake%20Plane%20Crash&match=1; https://www.syracuse.com/news/2012/02/boat_wrecks_on_bottom_of_onond.html

Oh My Darling Hill Observatory

Fadraga, Hector. "Syracuse Astronomical Society opens observatory for a look at heavens." *Syracuse Herald Journal*, April 7, 2000.; http://www.syracuse-astro.org/about-darling-hill-observatory/; http://www.syracuse-astro.org/scope-etiquette-tips-for-enjoying-public-observing-sessions-at-dho/; http://www.syracuse-astro.org/3d-flip-book/2023-brochure/.

Keep on Truckin' . . . Just Not Here

https://www.syracuse.com/crime/2022/03/yes-another-truck-just-hit-the-onondaga-lake-parkway-railroad-bridge.html; https://www.youtube.com/watch?v=mbeCzQvrDks; https://www.syracuse.com/news/2010/09/megabus_driver_was_checking_hi.html; https://www.syracuse.com/living/2022/04/the-untold-history-of-cnys-notorious-parkway-bridge-why-its-so-low-so-strong-and-so-stubborn.html.

Two Towers, Two Women

https://www.syracuse.com/news/2011/09/a_tour_of_world_trade_center_d.html; https://www.localsyr.com/remembering-9-11/dewitt-sculptor-revisits-her-9-11-remembrance-creation-from-twin-tower-beam/; https://www.waymarking.com/waymarks/wm4MPN_9_11_Memorial_Town_of_DeWitt_NY; https://obits.syracuse.com/us/obituaries/syracuse/name/patricia-masten-obituary?pid=192860411.

Area 315 and Explosive D

https://nyheritage.org/collections/new-york-ordnance-works-collection; https://eaglenewsonline.com/opinion/point-of-view/2017/04/17/baldwinsville-history-mystery-do-you-know-anything-about-this-picture-50/; https://www.nae.usace.army.mil/Portals/74/docs/Topics/FormerNewYorkOrdnanceWorks(NYOW)/NYOW-FactSheet-Aug2020.pdf; http://www.bville.lib.ny.us/wp-content/uploads/2020/01/Walking-Tour-of-Radisson-new-booklet.pdf.

Eerie on Erie

https://eaglenewsonline.com/new/2011/10/25/more-half-dozen-hauntings-detected-syracuse/; https://www.syracuse.com/strangecny/2007/10/third_stop_the_erie_canal_muse.html; https://eriecanalmuseum.org/gingerbread/.

Cuts like a Knife

Lief, Alfred. Camillus: *The Story of an American Small Business*. New York: Columbia University Press, 1944; https://www.camillushistory.org/landmarks/camillus-cutlery; https://www.syracuse.com/news/2013/02/camillus_cutlerys_factory_root.html; https://www.npr.org/2021/09/10/1035131619/911-travel-timeline-tsa; https://historyengine.richmond.edu/episodes/view/1410; https://woodsandarrow.com/camillus-cutlery-company-history/; http://www.collectors-of-camillus.us/History/camilluss.pdf; http://www.collectors-of-camillus.us/History/Camillus-Short-history.pdf; https://www.syracuse.com/news/2017/12/former_cny_knife_factory_converted_into_apartments_popular_coffee_shop_to_open_o.html.

We Are Family

https://www.timecapinc.com/our-projects; https://www.syracuse.com/cnyspeaks/2009/01/big_beautiful_house_smack_in_t.html; https://www.syracuse.com/opinion/2010/06/park_streets_five_sisters_find.html; https://www.syracuse.com/homes/2016/03/house_of_the_week_one_of_the_five_sisters_in_syracuse_a_castle_overlooking_leave.html; https://www.dunnedwards.com/pros/blog/the-painted-ladies-of-san-francisco/.

Put Your Foot in It

https://www.phrases.org.uk/bulletin_board/59/messages/486.html; https://invention.si.edu/charles-f-brannock; https://brannock.com/pages/about-us; https://www.syracuse.com/business/2019/05/central-new-yorks-brannock-foot-measuring-company-takes-nike-app-in-stride.html.

Furs, Explosives, Cadillacs, and Beer

Oser, Allan S. "About Real Estate: Radisson, an Upstate 'New Town' Near Syracuse, is Making Gains." *New York Times*, March 2, 1977, D9; https://timesmachine.nytimes.com/timesmachine/1977/03/02/76427727.html?pageNumber=79; "Schlitz Beer Company Completes First Brew." Syracuse *Post-Standard*, November 16, 1976.; https://newspaperarchive.com/syracuse-post-standard-jan-29-1980-p-17/; Greenhouse, Ezra. "Radisson Emerges as Settlement with Unity." *Syracuse Herald-American*, December 25, 1977; https://radissoncommunity.nabrnetwork.com/hoapage.php?page=-gen_40_2404; "Firm to Buy B'ville Site at $1 Million." Syracuse *Post-Standard*, August 22, 1968; "OIDC Offers to Purchase Ordnance Plant Site Option." Syracuse Post-Standard, May 28, 1969; https://newspaperarchive.com/syracuse-post-standard-jan-29-1980-p-17/; https://www.census.gov/quickfacts/radissoncdpnewyork; https://esd.ny.gov/radisson-community-project.

Art of Glass

https://icpompey.org/wp-content/uploads/Henry-Keck-Studios-Bio.pdf; https://vwpresby.org/stained-glass/history/; https://archivesspace.cmog.org/agents/corporate_entities/84; https://www.cnyhistory.org/2021/08/stained-glass-and-a-glass-of-wine/.

Strong Smell of Success

https://www.pharmaceutical-technology.com/projects/bristolmyerseastsyra/; https://www.syracuse.com/news/2010/06/at_bristol-myeres_squibb_plant.html; https://www.syracuse.com/living/2022/06/opened-during-wwii-bristol-myers-in-syracuse-was-the-worlds-biggest-penicillin-maker-by-1950.html; https://www.syracuse.com/business/2023/01/lotte-completes-purchase-of-bristol-myers-squibbs-pharmaceutical-plant-in-east-syracuse.html; https://www.ast.org/ceonline/articles/402/files/assets/common/downloads/publication.pdf; https://pharmaphorum.com/views-and-analysis/a-history-of-bristol-myers-squibb/.

More than Good Bones

https://patents.google.com/patent/US1421236A/en; https://www.concrete.org/publications/internationalconcreteabstractsportal/m/details/id/15507; https://www.facebook.com/ACSCNY/posts/paul-huebers-fireproof-homes-on-shotwell-park-syracuseas-we-keep-looking-at-more/10158733273066443/.

En-Gulfed by the Unknown

https://scarycuse.proboards.com/thread/84; https://bigfrog104.com/gulf-road-chittenango-ghost-haunted/; http://spearcases.blogspot.com/2011/09/gulf-road-chittenango-ny.html; https://www.newyorkhauntedhouses.com/real-haunt/gulf-road.html; https://www.hauntedplaces.org/item/gulf-road/.

Tiny Slopes

https://www.skicentral.com/fourseasonsgolfandskicenter.html; https://nccnews.newhouse.syr.edu/small-and-sturdy/; https://www.wmur.com/article/fresh-tracks-taking-a-tour-of-one-of-the-smallest-ski-areas-in-us/5195573; https://www.localsyr.com/news/local-news/mother-nature-having-an-impact-on-local-ski-resort/; https://www.fourseasonsgolfandski.com/home.

The Darling of Strathmore and Sedgwick

https://www.livingplaces.com/people/ward-wellington-ward.html; https://dd20century.tumblr.com/post/673422918/ten-things-you-should-know-about-architect-ward; https://pacny.net/onondaga-county-vacant-ward-wellington-ward-houses-2019/; https://www.syracuse.com/business-news/2018/08/; http://mycentralnewyork.blogspot.com/2017/12/moravian-tile-fireplace-revealed-in-w-w.htmldemolition_of_le_moyne_manor_a_liverpool_landmark_underway.html; https://www.syracuse.com/vintage/2016/10/check_out_26_syracuse_homes_on.html.

It's the Pits

https://www.trailforks.com/region/skytop-quarry-20431/?activitytype=1&z=14.0&lat=43.00590&lon=-76.09002; https://www.yelp.com/biz/skytop-quarry-syracuse; https://www.atlasobscura.com/places/skytop-quarry; https://www.syracuse.com/business-news/2015/10/could_these_rocky_ruins_turn_into_a_syracuse_jobs_creator.html.

A River Runs through It

https://creekrats.org; https://hiddenwatersblog.wordpress.com/2022/02/04/onondaga-creek-syracuse/; https://creekrats.org/enjoy-onondaga-creek/; https://fishonondagacounty.com/about-the-fishing/bodies-of-water/onondaga-creek/; https://www.syracuse.com/news/2011/08/no_traffic_lights_slow_his_com.html; https://www.syracuse.com/news/2022/09/meet-the-creek-rats-as-they-try-to-turn-a-stinky-syracuse-stream-into-an-attraction.html.

Are You My Mummy?

https://www.atlasobscura.com/places/cabinet-of-curiosity-at-cazenovia-public-library; https://www.cazenoviapubliclibrary.org/hubbards-legacy-exhibit/; https://www.cazenoviapubliclibrary.org/museum-gallery/museum/306-2/; https://www.syracuse.com/east/2009/05/cazenovia_public_library_unvei.html; "Death Came Unexpectedly: Robert J. Hubbard is Mourned in Cazenovia." Syracuse *Post-Standard*, December 20, 1904.

Heaven on Earth

https://www.gerritsmith.org; https://www.measuringworth.com/calculators/uscompare/relativevalue.php; https://www.influencewatch.org/non-profit/bill-and-melinda-gates-foundation/; https://www.uticaod.com/story/mid-york-weekly/2021/07/22/historian-presents-story-human-rights-crusade-peterboro-ny/8055493002/; https://www.wpbstv.org/the-gerrit-smith-estate-the-national-abolition-hall-of-fame-peterboro-new-york-wpbs-short-flix/; https://www.nps.gov/nr/travel/underground/ny3.htm; http://blogs.colgate.edu/upstateinstitute/files/2013/01/National-Abolition-HOF-Whitepaper.pdf.

Resistance in Black and White

https://www.history.com/topics/black-history/fugitive-slave-acts; https://www.cnyhistory.org/2014/10/jerry-rescue/; https://www.hmdb.org/m.asp?m=138797; https://www.zinnedproject.org/news/tdih/jerry-rescue/; https://pacny.net/freedom_trail/JerryRescue.htm; http://www.nyhistory.com/gerritsmith/jerry.htm; https://dailyorange.com/2022/09/171-years-later-jerry-rescue-day-local-attention-social-change-syracuse/; https://www.washingtonpost.com/history/2022/10/01/jerry-rescue-syracuse-slavery/; https://www.slaverymonuments.org/items/show/1171.

Sweet Spring or Haunted Hollow?

https://findaspring.com/spring/locations/north-america/usa/whiskey-hollow-spring-memphis-ny/; https://www.syracuse.com/news/2012/01/baldwinsville_teens_movie_expl.html; https://cnyhiking.com/WhiskeyHollow.htm; http://www.weirdus.com/states/new_york/road_less_traveled/whiskey_hollow_road/index.php; https://cnycentral.com/news/local/is-spring-water-safe-video.

Cheap Deals on Teall

https://lyncourt-grocery-outlet.business.site; https://www.facebook.com/lyncourtgroceryoutlet; https://www.syracuse.com/business-news/2015/10/plaza_that_housed_syracuse_china_outlet_making_a_comeback.html.

Duck, Duck, Goose

http://www.websterpond.org/index.html; https://cnycf.org/beyond-the-pond-the-deeper-role-of-webster-pond/; https://www.syracuse.com/outdoors/2012/06/chad_norton_makes_webster_pond.html; https://www.syracuse.

com/crime/2021/08/central-ny-community-rallies-to-raise-money-after-webster-pond-office-ransacked.html.

Unique and Far Away from It All

https://www.dec.ny.gov/lands/37070.html; https://www.syracuse.com/outdoors/2020/04/get-outdoors-exploring-labrador-hollow-unique-area-in-south-onondaga-county.html; https://cnyhiking.com/LabradorHollowUniqueArea.htm.

Roads to Nowhere

http://www.empirestateroads.com/week/week19.html; https://www.interstate-guide.com/i-690-ny/; https://www.alpsroads.net/roads/ny/i-690/; https://www.aaroads.com/guides/i-690-west-ny/#gallery-2; https://www.aaroads.com/guides/i-690-west-ny/; Graham, Ronald. "F'ville By-Pass Eyed." Syracuse *Post-Standard*, September 16, 1965.

INDEX